Assault

Assault

by EVA JOLENE BOYD

THOROUGHBRED
Legends®

No. 23

ECLIPSE
PRESS

Lexington, Kentucky

Library of Congress Control Number: 2003097835

ISBN 1-58150-107-2

Printed in The United States
First Edition: November 2004

Distributed to the trade by
National Book Network
4501 Forbes Boulevard, Suite 200
Lanham, MD 20706
1.800.462.6420

a division of
Blood-Horse Publications
PUBLISHERS SINCE 1916

ASSAULT

CONTENTS

INTRODUCTION

The Brasada

O ne day about forty years ago, I rode my horse, Jubal, along a fence line on a friend's cattle ranch near Falfurrias, Texas. The ranch, located about thirty-five air miles southwest of King Ranch headquarters, was a microcosm of its huge neighbor. It had much the same beauties, the abundance of wildlife and the gnarled trunks of live oaks, and it had the same problem with the ever-encroaching brush. Still, even the brush has its advantages. It gives refuge to all types of wildlife. In the mid-1880s these chaparral thickets hid longhorns from the cowboys who had come to round them up for the long one-way journeys up the cattle trails to Kansas.

Late afternoon wasn't a good time of day for my friend and me to be riding in the brush. The trail, much of it in shade, couldn't have been wider than five feet from the barbed wire fence on the right to a dense chaparral thicket on the left. This was the perfect time of day for brush country critters to come out. The first we came upon was a family of noisy javelinas, small wild pigs native to the Southwest, the adults of which sport tusks that can kill large dogs. At our approach, the javelinas squealed and grunted and moved surprisingly fast to melt into the darkest and densest part of the thicket.

No more than five minutes later I spotted a diamondback rattler stretched across the trail. This one was small as the western variety goes, barely half the six- to seven-footers that are common around here. I called back "rattler" to my companion, and we stopped to see what the snake was going to do — head on out to wherever it was going, turn around and hide in the cactus, or — as we expected — react to our presence by coiling and rattling, something that often sends a horse into orbit. But this one just stayed put and stayed silent, so I allowed Jubal to go on. If the snake reacted, we could wind up on the fence or in the cactus. Or on the snake.

Both horses stepped over the rattler without turning a hair. I took a last backward glance to see the snake crawling into the cactus.

I came away from this ride feeling rather privileged

to have been taken back in a kind of time warp. This place, the *brasada*, the brush country, has always been a place where the fittest, and sometimes the luckiest, survive and where adversity builds character.

History books show that in the spring of 1846, preparatory to the Mexican War, some 4,000 infantrymen led by General Zachary Taylor marched south from Corpus Christi, on the Texas Gulf Coast, to the Rio Grande. They arrived in late April and were soon scoring victories against Mexican soldiers at Palo Alto and Resaca de la Palma in the war's opening salvos. What you won't see in textbooks is that Taylor's army was attacked en route and nearly sent packing.

By a lone wild bull.

The animal had apparently been napping in the mottled shade of a chaparral and mesquite thicket, when the approaching army interrupted his siesta. He rose to his feet and likely would have retreated into the thicket if one of the soldiers hadn't fired his gun. The shot missed, but it got the bull's full attention. He wheeled and charged straight into the column. Well-trained soldiers scattered "like chaff," according to an eyewitness, and a near rout ensued as they charged into the

columns of men behind them, who, in turn, began shooting at what they believed was the Mexican army.

Miraculously no one was hit, not even the bull, which turned, and disappeared into the thicket.

The attack occurred somewhere along the Matamoros Road, an old trade route that ran northward from Matamoros, Mexico, to Texas settlements at Goliad, Victoria, and beyond. The first 165 miles passed through a large expanse of nearly uninhabited land that is still referred to as the Wild Horse Desert. "Of this section of country little is known," wrote the cartographers on an 1839 map in the General Land Office in Austin. And on another: "Immense Herds of Wild Horses or Wild Horse Desert." Future U.S. president Ulysses S. Grant described the country as teeming with "wild mustangs covering the plain clear to the horizon in three directions, too many…to be corraled in the whole state of Rhode Island."[1] The wild horses have long since disappeared, but the name has endured.

This, too, is the *brasada*, the brush country of south Texas, and in the spring of 1852, six years after Taylor's run-in with the bull, Richard King stood by a creek shown on maps as the Santa Gertrudis and in all directions saw land alive with possibilities. By some accounts it was dry that spring; by others, the prairie grass brushed the stirrups of King's and his companions' saddles. By any account the journey was a hard one, even in 1852. The Mexican War had ended four years earlier, forever determining the Rio Grande, not the Nueces River that Mexico had claimed, as the international boundary between the United States and Mexico.

The overland excursion was not one to be taken lightly, and most people traveled by ship between Corpus Christi and Brownsville. Otherwise, it was a good five to six rugged days on horseback over the Matamoros Road. When Richard King and his companions left the boggy *resacas* (river or creekbeds) and woody palmetto thickets of the Rio Grande behind, they were barely twenty miles on the road before coming to the Arroyo Colorado. The stream hid its deception well, appearing to be fresh water then revealing itself to be salt water and burning the parched throats of those it had fooled. In a dozen more miles King came upon the remains of the El Sauz ranch, deserted as were most of the old Spanish land grants. The road then passed through blowing sand, forming dunes that were

never in one place for long, and salt ponds, and, if the rains had been good, an occasional fresh water seep.

Near the journey's end, the travelers came to their first abundant and reliable fresh water source. Santa Gertrudis Creek rose in the Santa Gertrudis de la Garza land grant and flowed through the Rincon de Santa Gertrudis grant until it emptied into Baffin Bay. The creek had become a regular stop for travelers on the Matamoros Road, and so it was for King. What Richard King saw as he stood looking out from the creek bank was a sea of grass encroached upon by chaparral brush thickets and stands of stunted live oaks, perpetually bent westward by the sea breeze.

This kingdom of savannah-like grass captivated King, who saw endless possibility in its vast expanse. He set his stake there, and south Texas was never the same again. This story is about a racehorse born in the brush country many years after King developed the ranch that bore his name; it's about the horse's adversity and certainly the character that made him a champion. Like that bull that took on an army, Assault never backed down from a fight. And this in a decade that might have been the most competitive in racing's history.

CHAPTER 1

The King Ranch

In the mid-1930s a south Texas brush-country cattle rancher found himself in the midst of the Kentucky bluegrass and Thoroughbred racing. It wasn't what Robert Justus Kleberg Jr. had planned, but while searching for one thing, he had discovered another.

Kleberg Jr. had gone to Kentucky with a singular interest in improving King Ranch's working cow horses.

It wasn't a new idea. His grandfather, Captain Richard King, a strong-minded, broad-shouldered steamboat pilot from New York City, had known the importance of mounting his vaqueros on good, dependable stock. Shortly after buying 15,500 acres that lay squarely along Santa Gertrudis Creek for three hundred dollars in 1853, King paid twice that for a Kentucky stallion to upgrade his cow-horse stock. "Six hundred dollars, when land was selling for 25 cents an acre, was one heckuva lot of money," said Helen Groves, the captain's great-granddaughter.

While King and his partner, Mifflin Kenedy, built up their ranching business and supplied the Confederacy with beef and horses, the two men continued to operate their steamboat business, which they had bought from the U.S. government at the end of the Mexican War.

They eventually sold their steamboat operation in 1874 and devoted all their time to ranching. The men had divided their land to protect the interests of their families but remained partners as long as King lived. During this time they embarked on the first large-scale fencing of land in south Texas as a means of improving their breeding program.

King continued to expand his ranch holdings until, at the time he died in 1885, he owned 500,000 acres. He and Kenedy were the biggest ranchers in the West and had become recognized leaders in the cattle industry.

Following King's death, his widow, Henrietta, asked Robert Kleberg II to take over the management of King Ranch. After studying law at the University of Virginia, Kleberg II wound up in Corpus Christi, where he opened a law office. King had been so impressed with how the young and exceptionally able Kleberg II had beat him in a lawsuit that King became one of Kleberg II's clients. A year after Kleberg II came to manage King Ranch, he married Alice Gertrudis King, the land baron's youngest daughter.

Kleberg II, who had no ranching experience, adapted quickly to the task at hand. Whereas King had been the pioneer, Kleberg II was the builder. He accomplished much, including eradicating the Spanish tick, which caused a fever in cattle; digging the first of the artesian wells to bring water to the surface in an area where little enough lay above ground; and initiating the plans to upgrade the beef cattle and the working horses.

Robert Kleberg Jr. was born in Corpus Christi on March 29, 1896. From the beginning his heart lay with the ranch and the livestock, taking up where his father left off. Before Kleberg Jr.'s father died in 1932, he handed the reins of King Ranch over to his son.

When it came to upgrading livestock, Kleberg Jr. thought genetics was the way to go. He had studied genetics for two years at the University of Wisconsin and, he admitted, "not much of anything else. I wasn't interested in anything else."

Turf writer Edward L. Bowen described Kleberg Jr. as a "cowboy with a scientist's approach to breeding."

The Texan's passion for genetics led him to embark on something that had not been done in two hundred years: creating a new breed of cattle. The native long-horns had their day, when some ten million had been rounded up out of south Texas and surrounding areas and driven north to Kansas railheads from 1866 to the 1880s. But the ranchers were phasing them out. They were slow breeders, their meat was too lean for most northerners' tastes, and they were wild as deer. Most ranchers were importing beefy Herefords and English shorthorn. But these European varieties were unable to adapt to the hot south Texas climate.

"The area we were in," said Kleberg Jr., "is wonderful cattle country — with the right cattle. It was not such good cattle country for the British breeds."

After years of experimenting with the beefy short-horn and the heat-resistant Brahman, Kleberg Jr. created the cherry-red Santa Gertrudis, and in 1940 it became the first beef cattle breed recognized by the U.S. Department of Agriculture as being developed in America.

But Kleberg Jr.'s primary obsession was cow horses, particularly the Quarter Horse, which he wanted to return to its former glory. Curiously enough, a registry had never been established for the Quarter Horse, and by the 1930s the breed had lost many of its distinctive characteristics, particularly its compact, well-muscled body.

As far back as 1910, Kleberg II already had had the idea of infusing Thoroughbred blood into his range horses. That year he purchased thirty mares and two stallions from Sam Lazarus of Fort Worth, Texas. But for some reason these half-breeds turned out to be too nervous, too big, and too tall to be good working cow horses. The experiment didn't work that time; those horses were of poor stock, what cattlemen often referred to as "weeds."

On this subject Dr. J.K. Northway, the ranch's legendary veterinarian, once said: "The right kind of Thoroughbred blood never hurt any horse."

In a lengthy interview Kleberg Jr. told Bowen that "to produce any particular quality and, finally, to produce a whole bunch of characteristics that go together...the first thing you have to have are animals who are dominant in the particular thing that you want to produce.

"Say you get a good male — I do not care if it is a bull or Quarter Horse or Thoroughbred — you get that top animal, and you get a fair number of descendants. Then you can work through the sons and daughters of these animals for generations, and you keep trying to make little changes that you think would be advantageous. You get a big pool with that kind of genes...It is surprising how consistent they are after you get those characteristics concentrated in a certain number of males."

Kleberg Jr. is said to have been only nineteen when he chanced upon *the* horse. He had visited the farm of George Clegg, a breeder of both Thoroughbreds and Quarter Horses near Alice, some twenty-five miles from King Ranch. Kleberg was too young to have authority to buy stock for the ranch, but from a broodmare herd he singled out one mare and her sorrel colt and was determined to bring his cousin, Caesar Kleberg, back to see the pair. Caesar had as good an eye for horseflesh as the next Kleberg, and his attention immediately fell upon the same mare and foal. A little Texas horse tradin' and an exchange of $125 and the sorrel colt and his dam were led back to King Ranch. When the colt was weaned a few months later, the mare was returned to Clegg.

No one ever got around to giving the colt an official name; everyone at the ranch mostly called him the "Sorrel Horse," a nickname that later evolved into Old Sorrel. The $125 foal became the foundation stallion for King Ranch's famous Quarter Horses. The American Quarter Horse Registry was founded in 1940, the same year the Santa Gertrudis breed was being recognized, and Old Sorrel's grand champion grandson, Wimpy, was honored as the registry's first entry.

Kleberg never seemed to stop his quest for the right stallions. One, a Thoroughbred named Chicaro, piqued his interest in the 1930s and took him in a new direction.

"The story of our getting into the Thoroughbred game," he told Bowen, "was a sidelight of the Quarter Horse business." The rancher went on to tell about visiting his friend J.W. Dial's ranch and seeing "a very fine Thoroughbred horse that was a little different than any I ever had seen…he was bigger than I liked, but he had the same muscling that the Quarter Horse has."

Bred by one of racing's patriarchs, Harry Payne Whitney, the eleven-year-old Chicaro had impeccable breeding. His sire was the proven Chicle (by

18

Spearmint), and his dam, Wendy, was a daughter of the great Peter Pan. Looking up the pedigree, Kleberg felt his heart skip a beat. There was Commando (sire of Peter Pan), and through him was the Domino bloodline Kleberg admired, and so the Texas cattleman brought home a Thoroughbred stallion.

In the summer of 1935 he went to Kentucky. He wanted to "see how…a horse like that was produced." He wanted to meet the area's top breeders, and he wanted to see the mares and their foals turned out in their paddocks, and the stallions, if possible. He had a particular interest in horses with "Whitney blood," e.g. Chicle, Peter Pan, Broomstick, Hamburg, etc. But he also spent several days being driven down Lexington's wonderful little back roads and guided around farms.

As he arrived at Elsmeade Farm on Russell Cave Pike, Kleberg shouted to the driver (possibly Major Louis A. Beard, who managed the Whitney family's racing interests), "Stop the car! I see the mare I want!"

Among a group of fillies and mares owned by Morton L. Schwartz, Kleberg had spotted Corn Silk, a daughter of Chicle, Chicaro's sire. Just when Kleberg was thinking his luck bordered on eerie, he was told the mare was *not* for sale. At least not individually. Kleberg's disappointment lasted only as long as it took Schwartz, a New York breeder, to explain that his lease on Elsmeade Farm expired at the end of the year, and he was dispersing his breeding stock at Fasig-Tipton's Saratoga sales on August 21. Six-year-old Corn Silk and her Clock Tower foal were part of the lot of twenty fillies and mares going into the ring.

Kleberg did his homework before the sales. He walked the shed rows, looking at each horse from every angle like any veteran bidder. He talked with breeders and owners. He talked with trainers. Everyone agreed that as small as it was, Schwartz's consignment was still a real gem. Writing in *The Blood-Horse*, bloodstock adviser Humphrey S. Finney considered the lot as the best quality "presented before buyers since the [August] Belmont dispersal of 1925."

Almost before he realized it, Kleberg was bidding himself right into the racing picture. And at dispersal's end he had parted with $23,400, for which he obtained seven fillies and mares, including Corn Silk and her Clock Tower filly; Sunset Gun and her Peter Hastings colt; a Whichone—Footprint yearling filly; a Clock

Tower—Gun Play yearling filly; Science and her Whichone colt; and the Sir Gallahad III mare Easter. He paid another $16,000 for ten yearlings, bringing his expenditures to about $40,000 for the sale.

"It was almost a heist," wrote Bowen. "Right there, in front of the Saratoga regulars, the new man led off more good horses than most men own in a lifetime; enough good mares to start a breeding program that has stood the test of time." Bowen was right. Sunset Gun, the sale topper at $8,600, became the second dam of champions High Gun and Stymie; the Clock Tower filly turned out to be the smashing Dawn Play, Kleberg's first champion; and Science dropped a Santa Anita Derby winner in Ciencia.

"And, so," Kleberg told Ed Bowen, "I was in the racehorse business."

21

CHAPTER 2

Igual's Son

K leberg's enthusiasm about acquiring Chicaro stemmed from the speedy Domino blood on the stallion's dam's side. Kleberg considered the Domino line among the best in the country, if not the world, for performance, but the line was not necessarily always the soundest, especially through Domino's inbred grandson Ultimus (2x2 to Domino). So the Texas breeder began searching for a more hardy and sound branch of Domino blood and found it in Equipoise, a great-great-grandson of Domino through Pennant, Peter Pan, and Commando.

Equipoise fit Kleberg's idea of the proper type of stallion: big-bodied, powerful, courageous, and able to carry high weight at speed. Equipoise had retired in 1935 after six seasons of racing that included two seasons as Horse of the Year, a championship at two, and championships at four, five, and six. Equipoise raced fifty-one times, winning twenty-nine and placing in fourteen for earnings of $338,610. Among his major victories were the Suburban, Metropolitan, and Arlington handicaps, plus the Whitney Stakes, Hawthorne Gold Cup, Saratoga Cup, and Pimlico Futurity.

In looking for a well-bred mare to breed to Equipoise, who stood at C.V. Whitney's farm near Lexington, Kentucky, Kleberg came by the mare Incandescent. Bred by C.V. Whitney, Incandescent was out of Masda, a full sister to Man o' War, and by Chicle, the sire of Kleberg's earlier purchase, Chicaro. Incandescent began racing for the Whitney stable but was eventually claimed away. In three years of racing for various owners, she managed to win a claiming stakes and twelve other races in fifty-six starts. Major Louie Beard, who had been associated with the Whitney family's farms for many years, remembered the mare and recommended her to Kleberg.

During her broodmare career Incandescent would produce stakes winners Fuego and Flash Burn, but her first foal, the result of her union with Equipoise, must have loomed as a huge disappointment.

Foaled in 1937, Igual was a sickly looking filly, so small she looked less than full-term. "We had to hold her up while she was being suckled," Kleberg recounted in an interview with writer Frank Graham in the *Journal American* a few years later. "I thought for a while we would have to destroy her."

Igual was indeed on the verge of being destroyed, but, according to Kleberg, his cousin Caesar Kleberg asked that Kleberg wait and see if the filly would improve. "He (Caesar) is very patient," Kleberg told Graham, "and he kept watching her and studying her, and he asked me to give her a little more time."

A little more time didn't help Igual — pronounced Ih-wal and meaning "equal" in Spanish — and in fact only saw her slip further into debilitating weakness. Then one day, Caesar approached King Ranch veterinarian J.K. Northway. "Throw her down and go all over her, like we do the calves," Caesar told Northway, who had a good idea what Caesar was looking for. During branding, ailing or otherwise underweight calves are given a thorough hands-on examination, and the problem more times than not turns out to be an abscess of some sort.

So the little filly was put on her side. Dr. Northway examined her, and, sure enough, he found an abscess under her stifle. Caesar Kleberg must have been in attendance because "Mister Bob" told Graham that it was his cousin's suggestion to cut the abscess. "That's what we do with the calves, and it always clears up," Kleberg explained to Graham.

Although Igual recovered, she never gained her full weight. With the consensus that she couldn't withstand training but still had a valuable enough pedigree, she was placed in the broodmare band in 1939 at age two and was bred to Kleberg's first Thoroughbred stallion, Chicaro. The filly Equal Chance resulted from that union and went on to be a sturdy campaigner over five years. Igual was next bred to Equestrian, a Kleberg-acquired son of Equipoise, resulting in Masomenos, a non-winner in eight starts. Igual had no foal in 1942 but was bred that year for the first time to Bold Venture, another of Kleberg's stallion acquisitions.

Bold Venture had become part of the King Ranch operation in December 1939 when Kleberg paid $40,000 to Morton L. Schwartz for the horse.

A 1933 son of the imported St. Germans (sire of

1931 Horse of the Year Twenty Grand), Bold Venture was out of the Schwartz-owned Possible, a chestnut mare foaled in 1920. Her roots were solid, she being a daughter of Ultimus and out of a mare by the imported stallion Royal Flush III.

At some point in the early 1930s, Kleberg's path crossed with that of Schwartz' trainer, Max Hirsch. For sure they were at least acquaintances by 1935. That year Schwartz' colt Bold Venture ran through a so-so juvenile campaign, winning three of eight starts, and was unplaced in his only stakes attempts. But then Bold Venture was lucky to have even reached the races. A railcar in which he had been riding with several other two-year-olds filled with smoke from a smoldering fire, and only a quick-thinking groom holding the horse's head out a window had saved Bold Venture's life.

Bold Venture began his three-year-old season by winning an allowance prep for the Kentucky Derby. Oddsmakers weren't impressed, though, and for the Derby, he went off at more than 20-1. In a gritty performance, the colt beat favored Brevity by a determined head. Skeptics shrugged it off, pointing to the rough start that sent Brevity to his knees and had third-choice Granville losing his rider. Two weeks later Bold Venture proved the Derby was no fluke as he held off Granville in a slugfest down the stretch to win the Preakness Stakes by a nose. Here was a virtual unknown poised for immortality, but while prepping for the Belmont Stakes, Bold Venture bowed a tendon, and his racing career was over.

Schwartz sent Bold Venture to stud at Walter Salmon's Mereworth Farm near Lexington in the spring of 1937. Then in December 1939, Bold Venture was sold to Kleberg. In a letter to Kleberg dated January 4, 1940, Schwartz wrote that he believed Bold Venture to be "the most promising stallion in America. If he has any faults, I do not know of them."

Eighteen days later Kleberg received a letter from Dr. Robert Bardwell, the Mereworth farm manager. "I believe that BOLD VENTURE will get foals that will suit you especially well because I believe that you like heavy muscled blocky sort of horses." Bardwell assured him that Bold Venture's offspring tended to look like the stallion. Bold Venture was moved to John Hay Whitney's farm for the 1940 breeding season.

But breeders just weren't turned on. His female

family was not highly regarded and his conformation was nothing extraordinary, although that is presumably one of the things Kleberg liked about the horse. Bold Venture had more of a compact build, looking more like a sprinter than the stayer he was. Years later he would be described as being mistaken for a pony because he weighed less than a thousand pounds and didn't top 15 hands, 1 1/2-inches.

So Kleberg took Bold Venture home to south Texas, where he began the 1941 breeding season. Bold Venture would not become the hoped-for foundation for King Ranch as Thoroughbred breeder because of a tendency to sire soft-boned horses. The unsoundness, Kleberg admitted to *The Blood-Horse*'s Edward L. Bowen, "came through Ultimus, who was an inbred Domino horse."

However, in the spring of 1942 when he was bred to Igual, Bold Venture had only two crops on the track, so he still could be considered unproven at that point. From this mating a chestnut colt was foaled at King Ranch on March 26, 1943. He would be called Assault.

He had few markings, a small snip of a star on the forehead and a white left rear foot. He wasn't flashy, a

feature that most horsemen don't like anyway. His size was probably his biggest fault. But with that old saying, "the apple never falls far from the tree," the colt could have hardly been anything else given his sire's and dam's small statures.

Small or not, Assault had no self-esteem problems. In a few days he was turned out into one of the large mare-and-foal pastures, where he displayed just as much vigor as his bigger crop-mates. It wasn't long before Igual's son knew all the important places in his pasture. As bold as he was, he didn't venture into the dense thicket, which could hold many dangers. The mare-and-foal pastures were larger than their Kentucky counterparts with none of the precisely cut bluegrass and white wooden fences. The pastures at King Ranch were more natural and rugged, with a number of inherent dangers — rattlesnakes, armadillo holes, uneven ground.

Kleberg firmly believed that horses raised naturally in the open with a lot of roaming room were healthier overall than horses raised in stalls. "For some reason or other, I think horses raised in those big pastures and in that hot and dry climate are stronger. I don't know if they are sounder, but they are certainly stronger," he told Bowen in 1973.

Ironically, with all the dangers of the brush country, it wasn't one of nature's that struck Igual's son.

Survey workers were using wooden stakes to mark areas in the mare-and-foal pastures. When the surveyors went to clean the area, they missed one of the stakes in the tall spring grass, hidden also from the horses that roamed the pasture. Assault wouldn't have seen it, not until his right forefoot came down on the thing. The stake went through the frog or shock absorber of the foot and came out at the coronary band (hairline dividing the hoof from the bone structure above).

It was a grievous injury and an extremely painful one. Assault's quality of life looked pretty grim at this point. Kleberg loved his horses and never took lightly the decision to end one's life. But he saw a horse that was crippled and in pain and so, in a situation eerily parallel to that of Igual as a foal, he ordered the colt destroyed.

But the end result was nothing short of a miracle. One thing going for the little colt was that Kleberg was spending a lot of time out in the cattle pastures at the time. In short, he would be preoccupied for a while.

As he had with Igual, Dr. Northway stepped in to help. Northway was a third-generation Texan who grew up on a farm near San Antonio at the turn of the last century. The Northway name was well known in south Texas. His grandfather had fought with Sam Houston's army at the Battle of San Jacinto in 1836 to win Texas independence from Mexico. J.K. Northway had a particular love for horses and attended Kansas City Veterinary College, after which he went to work for King Ranch. This was in 1917, and except for serving in the Army Veterinary Corps during World War I, he would work for the Klebergs for many years.

As for Assault, Northway thought the foot could be saved as well as the colt's quality of life and had him and his dam moved into the veterinary clinic. Shortly thereafter, a severe infection set in, and the colt was in such pain he wouldn't put weight on that foot. Northway was left with a dilemma, then decided the spunky fellow deserved another chance. If the colt had inherited anything from his mother, let it be her powerful will to live.

In a drastic procedure Northway cut out much of the horny middle of the hoof. After that it was an around-the-clock ordeal. Fortunately, there were plenty of youngsters willing to help, such as Lolo Treviño and Martin Mendietta Jr., sons of King Ranch workers. Under the team's care the colt recovered.

Northway taught the boys how to apply gauze soaked with a special ointment. Lolo and Martin would diligently wrap the foot every morning to hold the medicated gauze on. Juan Silva, the ranch blacksmith, helped rebuild the split hoof.

As the foot healed, the next step was to get it to hold a shoe. It wouldn't be easy. It would never be easy. The hoof wall had become deformed, with the front hoof wall being only about an eighth of an inch thick. But Northway devised a piece of leather that fit between the hoof and shoe, holding the medicated gauzes in place. Eventually the gauzes and the pads were done away with, and the colt was fitted with a temporary shoe. The next step was getting him outside, letting him be a horse. He and Igual were put into a much smaller pasture.

Assault stepped gingerly into a world that was both familiar and held some memories of a terrible pain. As Northway and others watched, they could tell right

away there was a problem: He stumbled a lot. Occasionally, he fell. Just let him be, Northway said. As the summer heat reached its peak and then faded into milder nights and bearable days, the colt grew more confident. He still stumbled at a walk or trot, but when he moved into a lope, he was a horse again.

That fall when he was separated from his dam, the plucky youngster received his name. Bob Kleberg's wife, Helen, bestowed a name with power on the little fellow. Though the origin behind Assault's name seems lost, names evoking war and patriotism were popular in the 1940s.

Assault had bonded with his dam more so than usual, so their separation might have been more traumatic, but he and his fellow weanlings weren't given time to dwell on their loneliness. Human hands replaced their mothers' comforting actions. It was easier for Assault; he had long since bonded with the people around him. Having his feet picked up and fooled with was as much a part of the daily routine as hearing the rattle of feed buckets.

Assault's extra handling perhaps gave him an edge over the other youngsters as they began training.

Actually, it might be said, he was a wee bit spoiled. Not that everyone didn't give him an extra pat now and then, but it was Caesar Kleberg who slipped him an extra sugar cube. Anything the colt did was fine and dandy with the old bachelor and deserved an extra treat.

And during new experiences, if there were any scary moments, Lolo Treviño's familiar voice made all the little gremlins go away.

In 2003 Treviño was well into his seventies but still carried himself with a pride well deserved, and he still vividly remembered the little chestnut colt he helped take care of. His ancestors owned the old Spanish land grant before Richard King purchased it. His great-great-grandfather helped build Santa Gertrudis, the main house and headquarters on the hill. Like most of the boys who were either born on King Ranch or whose parents worked there, Lolo began working with horses as soon as he was old enough to sit on one. He looked forward each year to weaning time, for the boys of light weight and gentle hands were the ones who broke the youngsters.

Breaking a horse must not be confused with the old

western way of subjugating the horse with sheer brute force, when punishment meant pain and a reward was nothing more than a pat on the neck. That method most often left a horse broken of spirit and harboring a distrust of everyone; a horse no rider wanted to stake his life on. That old way went out with the mustangs on King Ranch. It made for good movie fodder, and bad horses.

In the new breaking process Lolo gradually accustomed Assault to the feel of a light weight on his back. First he would walk alongside Assault while reaching his arms over the colt's back; then he would place a saddle pad on Assault's back, followed by a small breaking saddle, lightly cinched. Assault came to know that even the awkward weight of Treviño draped over his back meant no harm. That's not to say Assault lacked a rebellious spirit.

"At first he wanted to buck," Lolo recalled with a smile. "But I was gentle with him. Just threw me once. He was ready to go all the time." Assault would have other boys working with him, but no one really disputed the given that he was Lolo's horse. Nor did Lolo hesitate when he smiled and said, "I broke Assault."

Martin Mendietta Jr. also worked with Assault,

whom his young caretakers dubbed "the slow-footed comet." When the weanlings turned to yearlings, they were moved to the training barn adjacent to the mile training track where they began the serious work. Kleberg had this track built on the pattern of Belmont Park, except for the salt cedars that formed the outside "fence." This was Kleberg's favorite time to spend with the youngsters, the first time he could see his breeding theories converted into something tangible. The year-lings' immediate future depended on whether they did or didn't impress their "boss."

Just a few months earlier no one would have mentioned Assault in terms of racing. For all practical purposes he should have been dead. Now here he was galloping with another yearling on the track. José Garcia, crouching and with his rear well off the saddle, strained to hold the colt in. Garcia had just recently become an exercise rider. In fact, left up to his own mind, he wouldn't have been up on Assault at all.

Garcia was fourteen when Lauro Cavazos, the first person of Mexican descent to manage a King Ranch division and for whom the broodmare division Lauro's Hill was named, spotted him sweeping out a garage. He liked the boy's slight build, an indication that Garcia would be more at home on the back of a horse than behind a broom. But Garcia told him he didn't know how to ride and really didn't care to learn. For a boy his age on King Ranch in the early 1940s, this was almost unheard of. Lauro finally convinced Garcia to try it, and the boy known as "Pie" Garcia became such a gifted exercise rider that he accompanied the young horses to New York each year to ride for trainer Max Hirsch.

As Assault grew up and grew stronger, so did his feistiness. Lolo Treviño described him as "desperate all the time, ready to go. He wouldn't stay still for anything."

In November 1944, King Ranch's trainer Max Hirsch arrived in south Texas to inspect the yearlings with Kleberg. Soon Assault's fate would be decided. Would Hirsch send him to the racetrack, and could his foot even withstand training? If anyone could prepare the little chestnut for the rigors of racing, it would be Max Hirsch.

ASSAULT

CHAPTER 3

"I was a whoop-dee-do rider"

The most momentous event in Bob Kleberg's life just might have been when he met Max Hirsch. The two men shared some almost eerie similarities — both were Texans, had German backgrounds, and shared middle names, at least phonetically: Robert Justus and Maximilian Justice. The two hit it off instantly and became the fastest of friends and confidants.

Both were from Texas but hewn from different soils. Following a straight line on a map two-hundred miles from King Ranch, one's finger traces over the Coastal Plains and Blackland Prairie, then up and over the Balcones Escarpment near San Antonio, and into the rumple of granite and limestone elevations of the Texas Hill Country to the small town of Fredericksburg. Max Hirsch was born there on July 30, 1880, in a little house that still stands on North Orange Street.

German immigrants founded Fredericksburg in 1845, bravely pushing beyond the line of civilization and settling in Comanche country. Hirsch once said he remembered when there were unfriendly Indians in the hills. But these settlers, a long way from any outside help, took the initiative and extended a hand of trust and friendship and, within a year of the town's founding, had a peace treaty with the Comanches.

An 1870 census shows Jacob arriving in Texas from Hamburg, Germany, while his wife, Mary, or Maria, is shown to have been born in Texas. The couple had six children. The four boys came first, with Max bringing up the tail end. Louis, the second eldest, told the Fredericksburg newspaper, the *Radio Post*, in 1956 that Max was a spirited youngster who liked nothing better than riding horses all out, from flag to flag.

"I was a whoop-dee-do rider," Max admitted years later to Turf writer Joe Hirsch in *The First Century* (DRF Press, 1996). "I went to the front as fast as I could, stayed there as long as I could."

Max Hirsch tackled most tasks all out, including riding the calves his grandfather raised on a farm near Cross Mountain about a mile north of town. "Max and a pal would go out to grandfather's and find some calves," Louis said in his story. "They roped and rode them. The calves bellowed and ran at top speed, throwing the boys in all directions."

But Max's first love was racing horses.

Louis, who was teaching in another town at the time, had a horse that the youngster would borrow to race on the weekends his brother returned home.

Hirsch was already an experienced rider by age eight. That was when he got his own horse, a pretty little black he saw tied in front of the Buckhorn Saloon in San Antonio. Max fell in love with the horse and begged Louis to buy it. Louis hesitated. *What if it's stolen? Well, it would be nice if Max had his own horse.* So Louis found the owner, who demanded twenty-five dollars. Louis laid twenty dollars on the table, all he had on him. The deal closed, and Max's new acquisition promptly kicked him squarely in the jaw.

No harm done. Some loose teeth. A sore jaw. Max was more concerned with what would happen if his father found out the horse had kicked him, and the eight-year-old made Louis promise not to tell.

The horse, despite its initial greeting, proved Max's

keen eye for horseflesh at an early age. "It turned out to be the best horse in that section," Louis told the *Radio Post*.

Over the next few years, several people noticed Max's riding skills at the local fair. By the time he was ten, Max was riding races for the county judge, the livery stable owner, and others, and he rode regularly on Saturdays and holidays, especially the Fourth of July.

During the local fair in 1890, a New Yorker named John A. Morris approached him. Morris had watched him ride and liked what he saw. The boy had strong hands and a fair sense of timing. He was almost fearless on the track and knew nothing except to slam-bang it to the front, that "whoop-dee-do" style Max himself referred to years later.

Morris knew talent and potential when he saw it. His family had one of the biggest racing stables in the East, their runners known by the famous "all-scarlet" silks. His father, Francis Morris, had raced many good runners, including the great racing quintet known as the "Barbarous Battalion," five full sisters all from the mare Barbarity and bearing such unladylike names as Ruthless (foaled in 1864 and winner of the first

Belmont Stakes), Relentless, Remorseless, Regardless,
and the last in 1873, Merciless.

In 1856 Francis Morris purchased 23,040 acres in
the south central Texas hills near Fredericksburg. Three
years later he sold 6,400 acres but apparently never did
anything with the rest. In fact, there is no indication he
ever visited the land. When he died in 1886, the land
passed to his son, John, and grandsons, A.H. and D.H.
Morris, who quickly transformed the property into a
self-supporting Thoroughbred breeding and training
center, only a few miles southwest of Fredericksburg.
The magnitude of what was there — some 16,000 acres
— made Morris Ranch a legend in the area.

Max was offered a job exercising their
Thoroughbreds. He would live there — the riders had
their own residence, a two-story stone house with the
lower floor given over to the kitchen, cook's quarters,
dining room, and recreation room; Max would continue his studies — Morris Ranch had its own school; and
he would attend church every Sabbath. The Hirsches
must have given it a great deal of thought; Max would
be supervised; the mile training track was considerably
safer than those "courses" the boys scratched out of

rocky pastures. *If this is what Max wants...*, they thought, *he'll see that taking care of horses all the time is hard work and he'll tire of it and learn a trade.*

Max later recalled those years with a bittersweet fondness. Yes, the work was hard. He didn't just exercise horses; the boys mucked stalls, walked hots, wrapped bandages, and kept up with their studies. By age thirteen, or twelve by some accounts, Max had set his mind to go east to Maryland or New York. That's where the big tracks with the big races and big purses were. He had even figured out how he would get there.

Once a year the Morrises picked yearlings to go east to trainer Wyndham Walden, generally about thirty from an annual crop of more than a hundred. The appointed horses were loaded onto railcars for the four-day journey from Texas to Baltimore. In the spring of 1893, as Max helped load the yearlings, the impulsive twelve-year-old got on board the train.

The only thing he hadn't counted on was the weather.

The day had begun cool enough for jackets as they loaded horses but had warmed up considerably, and Max found himself shedding some of his outer garments. The short of it being, when the train pulled away from the station, Max's clothes and shoes lay in a pile on the loading dock. Four days later the train rolled into Baltimore during a snowstorm. John Morris, who was in Maryland, probably received a telegram from Texas when Max's clothes were found and after a brief search discovered a very hypothermic boy huddling in a corner.

As Max sipped hot tea and soup, the youngster had to wonder what was going to happen next. Surprisingly, the Morrises allowed him to stay, and he worked as an exercise rider.

Many years after his clandestine excursion Max recalled that his first race as a real jockey was in 1894 at Morris Park in the Bronx. The John Morris-built track had opened in 1889. He was only fourteen, and with sixteen being the minimum age for a jockey's license, he "hedged" on that line. Being somewhat tall for his age helped. As he paraded on the Morris Park track — the longest in the country until Belmont Park opened in 1905 — Max knew he was where he belonged.

From a perspective of many years after the fact, Max knew it hadn't been all glamour and "whoop-dee-do." In fact, the horses suffered a great deal then by the misuse of whips and roweled spurs. The great Domino is said to have been so marked up by jockey Fred Taral that the horse had to be blindfolded to allow Taral anywhere near him. Officials often looked the other way when granting jockey licenses. So many horses were assigned eighty or ninety pounds, usually only younger boys were hired to make the weights. And then there were the tracks. Rain turned them into treacherous bogs. "Getting the horse back without falling was the big job," Max recalled in 1967 to *Daily Racing Form*'s Teddy Cox. "Winning was secondary. And you can imagine a little kid weighing about 70 pounds trying to steady a horse in that kind of going.

"They didn't have any child labor laws in those days and it wasn't at all unusual for horses to carry less than 80 pounds. I did 80 pounds with a big saddle."

Hirsch rode for five years before being grounded by weight. He booted home 123 winners from 1,117 mounts. Racing columnist W.E. Burke wrote in the *National Turf Digest*: "Maxie made a big reputation for himself on all the prominent tracks of the country, appearing almost entirely in the colors of [Wyndham] Walden and the Morrises."

A year after retiring from the saddle, Max Hirsch went out on his own as a trainer. He was just twenty.

The list of the good horses Hirsch trained reads like a "Who's Who," including two undisputed greats in Sarazen and Grey Lag, but a horse he both owned and saddled very early in his career remained a favorite. Beauclere was Hirsch's first stakes winner as a trainer; he had named the horse for his new bride of 1905, Kathryn Claire. This was more than just a nice colt who bore a special name. In his last start as a two-year-old in 1906, Beauclere beat older horses at ten furlongs and the following year won the Washington Cup at two and a quarter miles.

Gambling reform legislation closed the tracks for a while, but Hirsch showed he hadn't lost a step when they reopened. Always known for spotting youngsters with promising futures, Max picked up Norse King for only $275 from August Belmont and won eight races with him. He was Max's first Kentucky Derby starter, finishing fifteenth in Regret's 1915 renewal. The young trainer soon picked up a client in George Loft, of "Pound-a-Penny Profit" candy fame. Loft gave Papp to Max to train, and the horse won the 1917 Futurity.

Unfortunately, some of the horses he trained at the time, although gifted enough, had the misfortune of being in the same 1917 foal crop as Man o' War.

By 1935 Max Hirsch was among the deans of his profession. His public stable was one of the largest, his clients including the prominent Morton L. Schwartz. But when the decade was half-over, Schwartz decided to get out of the business and offered his racing fillies and broodmares at Fasig-Tipton's Saratoga sales in August. Racing can be a sport of fun and ironies. In dispersing his breeding operation, Schwartz sent Robert Kleberg Jr. home with an enviable beginning to his own Thoroughbred breeding future.

With his principle patron retiring, Hirsch faced a pivotal point in his life and career. But when he was hired as the King Ranch trainer, no one seemed too surprised. It was as if all the events of the past forty-five years had been falling into place all along, just to lead him to that point, back to Texas.

He and Kleberg would form a partnership and friendship that would remain strong for another three-and-a half decades.

CHAPTER 4

"This sounds fanciful, but it could happen!"

Each year around November Max Hirsch arrived at King Ranch to inspect the yearlings. He and Kleberg would view the young horses, then compare notes on which horses were to go where. Depending upon the horses' level of maturity and readiness, part of the yearling group would be shipped to Hirsch's winter base at Columbia, South Carolina, and then sent on to Hirsch's stable at Belmont Park prior to the track's summer meeting, while others would join Hirsch's son Buddy in California. These were the borderline horses, and Buddy Hirsch had a gifted way of developing some fair stakes winners from the claiming ranks.

The senior Hirsch may have first heard about Assault when Kleberg sent a letter in the fall of 1943, explaining that Assault's name had been inadvertently omitted from a list of good prospects the trainer would be getting. No mention of Assault's foot was made:

"4. Bold Venture—Igual. This is an extremely top colt and belongs in the [best] four of the colts, and is one of the top Bold Ventures."

Under a listing of all the 1943 foals to be shipped out was this entry:

"Bold Venture—Igual. This colt is very close to Equipoise in conformation and is a sound, tough-looking colt, one of the best Bold Ventures so far dropped on this ranch. He should be left in all classic 2- and 3-year-old races."[1]

When Hirsch saw the yearlings sent to him in Columbia, he was not expecting to see Assault among them, presumably after having learned about the colt's foot during his November King Ranch visit. "I never thought he'd train at all with that foot," Hirsch told sportswriter Joe Palmer. "I wondered why they sent him up from the farm."

Assault had earned his way in yearling trials at King Ranch under the supervision of Bill Egan. In a 1946 article by Frank Reeves for *The Cattleman*, Egan admitted there was nothing exciting about the colt at first, but he loved to run and did so at every opportunity.

And, Egan added, Assault was second best in the yearling trials.

So, as *Dallas Morning News* sportswriter Gary West wrote in a 1996 article on Assault: "There he was, in South Carolina, in the winter of 1945, an unlikely prospect learning to become a racehorse but learning first of all to cope with his handicap."

Before he could learn to cope with his handicap, Assault first had to keep a shoe on his foot. The only place thick enough for a horseshoe nail was at the back of the hoof wall, and it was an iffy place at that. Elsewhere the hoof wall was weak and soft. It sounded impossible. Max Hirsch turned to blacksmith John Dern.

The great equine artist Richard Stone Reeves once described Dern as being a sort of shabby-looking, stout fellow with a "noticeably missing tooth," a likely description for a man whose profession was on the dangerous end of a horse. But Dern was well known for working with problem feet. If he could keep Assault shod, the horse possibly would have a career on the track. So Dern devised a plate with a tip turned up in front, a feature that theoretically would help anchor the shoe on. Because of the lack of places to put a nail, it was important that the bad foot be shod sparingly. "One bad blacksmith," warned Hirsch, "who fails to make use of the scanty hoof wall might put Assault out of racing for months or even forever."[2]

Hirsch decided to send Assault on to Belmont Park and prepare his handicapped colt for the start of the track's summer meeting, which was to begin in June. He had no idea what would become of this experiment. The colt could very well get out there and in the hard pounding of competition the shoe would fail; the foot would fail; and it would all be for naught.

From the looks of things, however, as the calendar changed from 1944 to 1945, there was a strong possibility that no one would ever know of a horse named Assault. As the time neared for Hirsch to take the newly turned two-year-olds to New York, racing plunged into its darkest hour, this just four years after enjoying record crowds and record handles. After the bombing of Pearl Harbor on December 7, 1941, and America's entry into World War II, racing officials sought ways to aid the government's war effort. New York Racing Commissioner Herbert Bayard Swope devised a war-relief effort of donating percentages and entire profits during meetings. Racing's contribution in 1942 amounted to $3.19 million and surpassed that amount the next year with more than $5 million. In October 1943, twenty-eight-year-old Exterminator's appearance at Belmont Park sold some $25 million in bonds. Closed tracks, such as Santa Anita, became internment camps or drill sites. Several tracks consolidated their meetings, including Belmont Park, which hosted Saratoga's races for three years to reduce wartime travel.

Then, in December 1944, James F. Byrnes, the director of War Mobilization and Reconversion, lowered the boom. He issued a "request" that all racing cease as of January 3, 1945, as well as all track operations, horse transportation, etc. "I urge that management of these tracks take immediate measures to bring present race meetings to a close by January 3, 1945, and to refrain from resuming at all tracks until war conditions permit," stated Byrnes.[3]

This did not set well with the racing community since Byrnes had only called upon horse racing to make such a sacrifice. And Earl Ruby, journalist and editor of the Louisville *Courier-Journal*, made no bones about it.

"As spring nears," he wrote in *The Thoroughbred Record* of March 10, 1945, "the fan in the street wonders if James F. Byrnes, the war mobilizer, is attempting to mobilize our morals as well as our manpower and transportation facilities...Basketball is going pell mell from coast to coast, with nation-wide tournaments coming up this month in Missouri and New York...Baseball, day and night; golf tournaments and exhibitions, bowling, billiards, and so on...Racing wasn't told to cut down 25 per cent, or 50 per cent, or 75 per cent...It was clamped shut like a vise."

Earlier, Neville Dunn, also writing in *The Thoroughbred Record*, had proposed that horsemen walk their Kentucky Derby entries to Churchill Downs from Lexington, a distance of eighty miles. The walk, of course, would be split up into certain mileages depending on what farms along the way would be willing to put the horses up for the night. "Twelve miles to Versailles" on that first day, wrote Dunn. "The second day they could walk the 12 miles or so to, say, Charlie Black's Silver Lake in Franklin County. The third day they could extend the march some 20 miles to Shelbyville." There were sufficient farms in the final thirty miles, and Dunn wrote, "This sounds fanciful, but it could happen!"

Fortunately, it never came to that. On Easter Sunday, March 31, James Byrnes recommended to President Franklin D. Roosevelt that the racing ban be lifted on V-E Day. Two days later, on April 2, Byrnes tendered his resignation and was succeeded by a Kentuckian. "I can say this for the owners of tracks and the owners of horses," Byrnes said good-naturedly in a press conference, "they were always good sports about closing down on racing...After all, I never issued the 'order.' I only requested a closedown on race tracks...But I am some requester," he added with a grin.

On May 7 Germany capitulated. The racing ban was lifted on May 9. Narragansett Park reopened on May 12; Santa Anita, three days later. Since the war with Japan raged on, more than 76,000 fans purchased war bonds as admission to Santa Anita. On that same day record crowds poured into Jamaica and Delaware Park. The Kentucky Derby was late, but it was run on June 9. The war ended in late summer, and racing fans continued to purchase bonds and file into the tracks. And finally Assault was able to make his presence known.

Not even a cloudy, rainy day could dampen the spirits of the crowd on Belmont's opening day on Monday, June 4. The fourth race on the card, with twenty-one starters, was a maiden four and a half-furlong sprint down the Widener Straight Course. Assault, with Jimmy Stout on board, drew a great deal of attention when he stumbled going to the track and nearly went down. The crowd murmured. *Isn't that horse lame? What is he doing running?* Regardless, Assault got some play at the windows. His odds of 17-1 were quite respectable for a first-time starter that couldn't walk very well. Three others went off at longer odds.

The chart noted that Assault showed an even effort. Breaking from the thirteenth post, he was eighth at the flag, then fell to eleventh and finished one more spot back. It would be the worst finish, in regard to position, of his entire career.

For Assault's next start eight days later Hirsch called on jockey Warren Mehrtens. The instructions were simple: Don't let him drop so far back. Hirsch was still learning what this colt wanted to do. This time the bettors thought the King Ranch entry should have stayed in the barn and sent him off at less than 79-1. This time, in a field of fifteen maidens, Assault finished fifth, missing a top-three finish by a length and three-quarters.

Hirsch put blinkers on him for the first time on the final day of the Belmont meeting. Again going four and a half furlongs down the Widener Course, Assault this time faced twenty-two other starters. He had been anything but fortunate in post-position draws so far. Thirteenth, twelfth, and today, sixteenth. But he was learning, and the blinkers made him focus. This time he held a one and a half-length lead at the quarter pole, which he reached in :23 1/5. Only in the final furlong did he lose the lead, to the highly regarded Mist o' Gold, one of the better juveniles of the year and owned by Vera Bragg. In finishing second Assault did bring home a slice of the pie, $580.

The racing action moved to Aqueduct for the July 12 Gowanus Purse at five and a half furlongs. Assault's effort meant more than finally finishing in the money. The fans had finally decided he wasn't going to fall flat on his face during the race and actually sent him off the third choice at nearly 5-1. He broke well from the second spot and showed an early turn of foot, getting the first quarter in :22 3/5. When Wheatley Stable's co-favorite Merry King came up and took the lead from him, Assault came back to win by more than a length for the $1,915 winner's share.

Assault was unable to make it two in a row in his next start, the six-furlong East View Stakes at Jamaica. He broke fifth and finished fifth, eight and a half lengths behind the winner Mist o' Gold.

His next start fell on a significant date in history.

The Belmont track was sloppy for the August 5 Flash Stakes at five and a half furlongs. Mist o' Gold headed the field of a dozen starters, but Assault looked steady with the resolve to match. Mehrtens settled Assault just off Manipur's pace during the cavalry charge down the Widener Course. Assault took the lead then discovered he had a scrap on his hands to keep it. Four finished under a blanket and Assault's nose poked in front for the $11,505 prize. His victory at 70-1 was quite a popular one, especially for those who cashed in two-dollar tickets for $143.20. And on the other side of the International Date Line, a lone B-29 Superfortress dropped one atomic bomb upon Hiroshima. In a few days the war in the Far East was over.

Assault lost his last three starts of the year. He hung in the six-furlong Babylon Handicap on September 5 to finish third. Behind him finished a new rival, Lord Boswell. In the six and a half-furlong Cowdin Stakes at Aqueduct on September 12, he was sluggish in the early going, then improved his position to finish fourth behind some good runners headed by Knockdown. The season ended on October 8 at the old egg-shaped Jamaica course in a six-furlong allowance. This time Assault gave Lord Boswell too much leeway and couldn't catch the Maine Chance Farm starter.

With a record of two wins in nine starts and $17,250 in earnings at two, Assault accompanied the rest of the stable to Columbia, South Carolina, where Hirsch worked with him slowly over the winter. Hirsch worked to build up his stamina, for in the Flash Stakes the colt had been running on fumes. The Experimental Free Handicap rankings at the end of the season indicate how the "experts" view the season, and Assault, as unimpressive as his numbers would appear, came out with 116 pounds, a figure that placed him in the eighteenth spot. Hirsch began to believe that Robert

Kleberg indeed knew his subject in that letter from two years earlier: "This is a sound tough looking colt...He should be left in all classic...3-year-old races."

CHAPTER 5

Oregon Boots

O ne sign of success in racing occurs when reporters start trekking to a barn that has been mostly uncharted territory.

That's not to say no one knew where Max Hirsch's barns were located at Belmont Park. They had been visited many times, if for no other reason than to be rewarded with a cup of Virgie's coffee and to watch the latest coin-hunting exploits of Homely the dog. It's just that Assault hadn't drawn too many serious folks, mostly just the curious to take a peek at the most famous foot in racing. But now that the little colt had proved that he wasn't a freak, that he wasn't going to fall flat on his face during a race, and that he might actually be good, reporters started coming around. Not a Man o' War-type line to be sure, but a steadily growing stream.

Popular sportswriter Joe Palmer found Assault the first part of April 1946. Nearby, Max Hirsch sipped coffee in front of his frame cottage on Belmont Park's backstretch. When Palmer arrived, Max called his cook, Virgie Malin, to bring another cup. Virgie was well known for her bracing java, and Palmer was looking forward to it on this cool spring morning. Homely, a big, black mongrel, wagged his tail then put his head down on his front paws. The boss would let him know when it was time to do his stuff.

Unlike most trainers, whose morning nutrition consists of doughnuts chased by coffee, Hirsch would rise at 4:45 every morning, watch a set or two work out, and then enjoy his usual breakfast of eggs, pancakes, sausage, grapefruit, and — he was a Texan — hot grits laden with butter, maybe a little sugar. Afterward he would return trackside promptly at six o'clock. After sending the last of his youngsters to gallop, Hirsch checked legs and feet for any heat, swelling, or, in Assault's case, missing shoes.

All in all Assault appeared to be progressing. He could run in the mud, he didn't quit when dirt was thrown in his face, and he could throw in some speed from any part of the racetrack.

And he continued to run true. Though he sometimes stumbled at a trot or a walk, once Assault leveled
out into a gallop, that unsteadiness disappeared into a
smooth stride. Some twenty-five years earlier Hirsch
sweated buckets every time Grey Lag took his shelly
hooves to the track, wondering if he would come back
with all four plates on. Now he had to worry all over
again with Assault.

This year would be more worrisome than last.
Assault had naturally put on a few pounds. The races
would be longer; weights, higher. Three-year-old cam-
paigns were tough, even on sound runners. Joe Palmer
thought all year that the foot looked as though it might
go out on the colt at any time.

For the most part, Max Hirsch had a good rapport
with the media, though a few reporters regarded him
as a "crusty curmudgeon," or in the case of David
Alexander, "an opinionated old rooster." Hirsch took
the jabs with his usual sense of humor, or he ignored
them. When it came to wanting it well known in the
racing circles that Assault was not club-footed nor was
he in pain, it was the respected Palmer whom Hirsch
invited to his barn that April morning.

As Palmer watched, a groom sponged the bad foot, careful to remove all the dirt and sand, then picked up the other front foot so Palmer could see the difference. Had Hirsch been skeptical when he saw the colt? Palmer wanted to know.

"When he came up from Texas," Hirsch began, "I didn't think he'd train at all. But he's never shown any sign that it hurts him. When he walks or trots, you'd think he was going to fall down. I think that while the foot still hurt him, he got in the habit of protecting it with an awkward gait, and now he keeps it up. But he gallops true."

On examining it more closely, Palmer thought the frog had a proper shape and all, but "it looked dry and desiccated, like a piece of very old, dry wood which keeps its shape but seems to have no solidity. It didn't look normal, but it didn't look sore either. The hoof was shod with a normal racing plate, except that a tip, about an inch long and a half-inch high, turned up in front to help anchor it on."

Thoroughbreds are normally shod every few weeks, so was Assault, on every foot but the bad one. As long as that plate presented no problems, it wasn't touched.

But Hirsch admitted that Assault had had to have it shod back in October and that it "was four days before we could get a plate to stay on."

To prevent a bad shoeing, only John Dern, who had devised the front tip on Assault's shoe, had permission to touch the colt's feet.

Before he left, Palmer likely asked whether Hirsch's dog really climbed trees.

No one knew exactly what Homely was, except that he was most assuredly a dog. Some said he was part Labrador; some said he was just typical of the American canine melting pot. Some said he wasn't normal. Max could tell you that he had more visitors to see Homely than any horses in the barn. "Besides climbing trees," said Hirsch, "he can track a half-dollar through a brush fire." Lacking the latter, Max would take hold of the dog's collar and tell his visitors to go behind the barn, where the horses graze, and drop a quarter or half-dollar into the tall grass. Moments later, Max would turn Homely loose, and as steady as a bloodhound, the dog would zero in. Then, after performing his tree-climbing shtick, the big dog contented himself with just being an ordinary barn mascot again.

Fourteen years later the sports columnist Red Smith visited Hirsch's barn to see Homely. Now Homely had long since climbed his last tree, but no one had ever discouraged his romantic inclinations, and Homely had stamped his looks onto several lanky pups. Max pointed out four of them: Homely II, Handsome, Tres, and Junior. That was all nice, but Red Smith was interested in the horse by the same name.

Just the previous week the equine Homely galloped to an easy win his first time out, a six-furlong claiming race for maidens three and older. Many people who remembered seeing Homely, the dog, climbing trees had just one question about Homely, the horse:

"No," Hirsch said, "he doesn't catch quarters and he hardly ever climbs trees, but he can run a little faster than the dog."

Besides the usual anticipation of any new year, 1946 looked to be a special one. For the first time in years, the United States wasn't at war. Max Hirsch had mixed emotions, however. His son, Harold R. Hirsch, had been killed in the Pacific in 1943.

One by one racetracks resumed their schedules, and two new ones opened on the Eastern Seaboard:

Monmouth Park and Atlantic City. The Kentucky
Derby for the first time was offering a $100,000-added
purse. So were the Preakness and Belmont stakes.

More horses were taking to the skies. Two had been
flown from Los Angeles to San Francisco for the Bay
Meadows meeting in late October 1945. One of these
first equine passengers, El Lobo, went on to win the
Burlingame Handicap on Bay Meadows' opening day.
By June 1946, four Thoroughbreds had been flown
internationally for the first time, from Mexico City to
Chicago. By November, a world record was set when
three horses were flown 8,250 miles from Buenos Aires
to Newark, New Jersey, in fifty-two hours. On
November 26 six horses were unloaded at Burbank,
California, less than thirty-six hours after taking off
from Shannon Airport in Ireland. Now racing secre-
taries, said Palmer, "would have to watch their condition books; merely knowing the horses were on the
grounds was no longer enough."

The year also saw its share of tragedies. On just the
third day of the year, popular jockey George "the
Iceman" Woolf died in a racing accident at Santa Anita.
Later in the year an equine sleeping sickness hit King

Ranch and claimed Equestrian, sire of the Max Hirsch-bred Stymie, and came close to taking Bold Venture as well. Also at King Ranch, Incandescent, Igual's dam, died after eating toxic clover.

Assault began the year on a winning foot, however, carrying 116 pounds in the six-furlong Experimental Free Handicap Number One on April 9. The race favorite and high weight was Mrs. John D. Hertz' Count Speed, but the full brother to 1943 Triple Crown winner Count Fleet took himself out when he reared in the starting gate and fell underneath. Mrs. Hertz' colt was extricated from his predicament and allowed to start, but, shaken up, he ran badly. Assault was in the adjoining stall, but if the incident bothered him, he didn't show it. Sent off at 9-1, he won under light restraint by four and a half lengths.

Rather than run Assault in the second Experimental Handicap, Hirsch opted for the mile and one-sixteenth Wood Memorial at Jamaica on April 20. The Wood, a considerably more prestigious and rich race, would indicate the kind of racehorse he had just two weeks before the Kentucky Derby. Assault would be going farther than before and carrying the classic weight of 126 pounds. At odds of less than 2-1, Hampden headed the field of fourteen starters. Assault, again running at a price — just under 9-1 — won by two and a quarter lengths.

Until Assault's win in the Wood, jockey and New York native Warren Mehrtens had been less than gung ho about referring to his mount as great. "Just another horse from the King Ranch," one writer quoted him as saying. And following the Wood? "He's a good horse, but not good enough for me to win the Derby, certainly not the Triple Crown." It was this less than cock-sure confidence in Assault that would later that year cause the kid from Brooklyn some regret.

As for Assault, this unknown, gimpy-footed colt from the south Texas hinterlands was two-for-two on the year and perched on the brink of immortality. As incredulous as it would have seemed less than two years earlier, the colt sentenced to death to prevent a lifetime of crippling pain was put on a train for Louisville with a legitimate shot at winning the most coveted race in the country.

First, on Tuesday of Derby week, there was the Derby Trial. Many trainers used its mile distance as a

final work before the big dance. This time it rained. And rained. But Assault had handled the mud before. He probably would have this time, if it hadn't been for those infernal Oregon Boots.

These leather and canvas wraps are attached with buckles around the lower hind legs and provide protection from interference by the hind feet. They might work just dandy under normal conditions. But hardly had Assault gone ten strides before the "boots" became saturated with mud and water. For Assault, who finished fourth behind Rippey, Spy Song, and With Pleasure, it must have felt like he was dragging the starting gate.

It wasn't widely known at the time, but Assault had a tendency to strike himself behind, hitting the inside of each leg with the opposite shoe. He also would hit his forelegs with his rear feet. Therefore, he usually ran with small adhesive bandages inside his hocks, plus a long bandage down his left fore cannon, often visible in winner's circle photographs. This time, as an extra precaution, Hirsch had added the Oregon Boots to the colt's hind legs. One observer was overheard to say, "Tis strange equipment for a horse that must race in the mud."

Reasonable minds would have thrown this race out without a second thought, but, instead, Assault's critics used it to legitimize their earlier claims that he wasn't classic material. His odds on that first Saturday in May when the windows closed that afternoon would increase from nearly 5-1 in the Trial to 8-1.

Hirsch blamed no one but himself. "I lost the race, not Assault," he was overheard saying several times. Then he put it behind him and reworked his plans to get Assault ready for the Derby.

If Robert Kleberg was disappointed in the Trial result, he didn't let it show, nor had the big victory "shindig" confidently planned for Saturday been dampened any by Assault's effort.

No doubt, though, that Kleberg mourned the loss on April 14 of Caesar Kleberg at age seventy-three. More than a cousin, Caeser had been Robert's mentor and friend for more than thirty years.

From the moment that Caesar had made the suggestion that saved Igual's life, to the efforts he had put in to likewise save her son, Caesar thought of himself as Assault's special guardian angel. To the other horses he handed a single sugar cube. To Assault, he gave two.

70

Caesar would have been the first to insist everything go as planned, especially if "his" colt won.

Caesar Kleberg surely would have reveled in the sheer numbers that converged on Churchill Downs for the seventy-second Kentucky Derby. The turnstiles began cranking around seven in the morning, and by that afternoon an estimated 105,000 fans packed the infield, grandstand, and apron, all under dark and threatening skies. Unless the sun appeared to dry the track out some, the surface would be listed as heavy for the five o'clock race.

One thing was certain: Assault would not be wearing Oregon Boots.

ASSAULT

CHAPTER 6

"It wasn't Assault. It was murder!"

The week leading up to the 1946 Kentucky Derby week was a festive time in Louisville, made more so by its being the first Derby since the war had ended. Churchill Downs president and general manager, Colonel Matt Winn, had increased the race's purse to $100,000 for the first time, and he confidently predicted a crowd of at least 100,000. The week was chock full of parties and parades; locals and visitors alike always had something to do, somewhere to go. If a person rated a coveted invitation to an elite Derby party, he or she could rub shoulders with a Vanderbilt or a Whitney. But even regular Joes had plenty of shindigs to choose from.

The King Ranch contingent arrived aboard two private planes, flying from Kingsville to Lexington. They then rode over to Louisville in a limousine the morning of the race.

One of the Derby parties took place at the Waldorf Astoria of Louisville (later the Brown Hotel) in the owner's suite on Friday night. After a few hours of freely flowing mint juleps, the hotel owner stood, not too steadily, and ssshhh'd everyone. "I have a surprise announcement," he said and waited for quiet. "It's common knowledge," he began, "I'm building a new cocktail lounge in the hotel. What you don't know is the fact I'm going to name the lounge after the winner of tomorrow's Derby. I promise you."[1]

Meanwhile, one Derby horse owner had tragic news to contend with.

Elizabeth Arden Graham, owner of a cosmetics firm as well as the famed Maine Chance Farm, had arrived in Louisville two days before the Derby. Her promising juvenile colt, Jet Pilot, was making his career debut on the Derby undercard, and her three-horse Derby entry led by the pre-race favorite, Lord Boswell, had most experts predicting at least a one-two finish. But the core of her Maine Chance two-year-olds, as well as Beaugay, the 1945 juvenile champion filly, and War Date, one of the leading three-year-old fillies of 1945, were stabled at Arlington Park in Chicago. Fire struck that Thursday night, taking twenty-two of Mrs. Graham's two-year-olds. Only Beaugay and War Date were saved. By Saturday investigators had traced the fire's origin to an electric heater left running in one of the stalls.

Mrs. Graham resisted going to Chicago. Those lost were beyond help; the two survivors weren't seriously injured and were in good hands. On Saturday, Jet Pilot eased some of the pain by easily winning the Dixiana. And her three-horse entry in the Derby continued to draw the most action at the windows.

The Klebergs were totally caught up in the Derby week spirit. The Running W on the King Ranch silks was still a bit of a curiosity with the Kentucky crowd whose main knowledge of the ranch was that it seemed to take up a good bit of south Texas. King Ranch's only other Derby starter had been Dispose, who finished sixth in 1941. In a sport in which fans are accustomed to silks adorned with sashes and dots and squares, diamonds, and hoops, the King Ranch silks showed the ranch's brand, the Running W, which dated back to the late 1860s. Richard King had given his brand a lot of thought. Not only were designs with sharp corners easy for rustlers to alter, but they could also cause hot spots that burn skin as well as hide on the animal. Finally, King settled on the wavy W, which the Mexicans called *El Vibrito,* or "Little Snake." Assault would soon be parading the brown silks with the cream-colored Running W before the record Derby crowd.

In 2003 Helen Groves, Helen and Robert Kleberg Jr.'s daughter, recalled her experiences on the day:

"The 1946 time was a wonderful, happy time. Soldiers were home. There were more people at the Kentucky Derby than ever before. And everyone dressed up to go to the races. We wouldn't think to wear shorts. The ladies wore gloves and hats and patent leather shoes."

Helen was a freshman at Vassar College at the time and had been invited to stay with a friend in Louisville. But even young ladies from Vassar weren't immune to the futility of trying to get through a record crowd to the betting windows. "We tried to get to the pari-mutuel windows," she said, "but the crowd was so bad we went to my family's box instead." The day's being wet and muddy didn't help matters; those patent leather shoes really took a beating.

Some young men from Yale who were sitting in the adjoining box came to the girls' rescue. It just so happened they were football players. "Come with us," one young man said, extending a hand. "We'll run interference for you so you can get your wager in."

Among the King Ranch party was Mary Lewis Kleberg, the wife of Robert Jr.'s nephew, Richard Kleberg Jr. She wasn't sure she should come, having just given birth six weeks ago to her fourth child, whom she was still nursing. So she put the question to her doctor, whose answer was short and sweet: "All right, you've given him a good start. Put him on a bottle and go."[2]

This was to have been the first nationally televised Kentucky Derby, twenty-one years after the first network radio broadcast took the race into living rooms. But a labor dispute between the Columbia Broadcasting System and the International Association of Theatrical and State Employees wasn't resolved in time.

Back at the ranch the vaqueros, including Martin Mendietta Jr., who had helped care for a young Assault, gathered around Dick Kleberg Sr.'s car to listen

to the broadcast. They anxiously awaited any word about Assault or possibly to hear their boss' familiar voice. Then through the static came the first notes of "My Old Kentucky Home," sounding so otherworldly out there on the Wild Horse Desert.

As the first notes of "My Old Kentucky Home" played, the Derby horses emerged from the tunnel and stepped onto the track. Assault, second to come into view, stopped and began looking around. He wasn't being ornery; he was only being a Thoroughbred. They're a curious breed. The great Australian galloper Carbine used to bird watch on his way to the track and woe betide the rider who tried to hurry him. Gallant Fox was fascinated by airplanes, which were something of a novelty in 1930. It's said that if a plane appeared overhead while Gallant Fox was on the track, he was like a wide-eyed kid who dreams of becoming a flyer. Those who have the look of eagles, it seems, are the most curious about their world.

"He wasn't spooky," Warren Mehrtens said of Assault's little quirks, "and if you let him look, he was never any trouble; but if you tried to hustle him, he could get rank."[3] Assault did move on without holding up the party. Fans watched him with a great deal of curiosity. Would he stumble on the way to the post?

Up in the Hirsch and Kleberg boxes, nerves were naturally on edge. Hirsch looked his same dapper self, his hat sitting at a jaunty angle. In many areas of the sports world, superstition forbids changing major habits right before the biggest game or race. But Hirsch this day was wearing a new suit and a sharp-eyed friend noticed a rabbit's foot dangling from a pocket. "You're too good a trainer to need that," the friend said. Hirsch smiled and explained that the good luck charm had been a Christmas present.

There were seventeen runners this day, and fans couldn't recall a more wide-open field. Knockdown, the Santa Anita Derby winner and a son of the great weight-carrier Discovery, had been the early winter-book favorite. But the role of pre-race favorite had passed to Knockdown's stablemate, Lord Boswell, the Blue Grass Stakes winner. Knockdown and Lord Boswell, who with Perfect Bahram comprised Mrs. Graham's entry, were less than even money by post time, with Foxcatcher Farm's Hampden the second betting choice at nearly 6-1 and Dixiana Farm's front-running Spy Song next at nearly 8-1. Assault's odds closed at 8-1; the other horses in the field were in double digits.

The horses reached the starting gates at 5:17 p.m. Central Daylight Time. The surface was upgraded to slow rather than muddy as it had been for the earlier races. But the skies darkened appreciably right before the Derby and looked as though they would dump a flood. Their parade and warm-ups over, the horses filed behind the starting gate where head starter Ruby White and his assistants took over.

Horses with a history of bad post manners were marked on White's program, a sort of "rap sheet." But the day, some who didn't have that history were acting up. Assault was the first to back out but was quickly reloaded. Then it was Jobar and Alworth. Jobar continued to act up even after being reloaded. This activity encouraged Knockdown and Dark Jungle to try for an early start. Finally, White gave the last two named barely seconds to face forward, then pressed the button.

A hundred thousand voices rose as one as the field broke cleanly. There were some very noticeable "yee-haws." Texans had made their way to Churchill Downs from the four corners of the country, their presence evident by the ubiquitous Stetsons and ropers and Levis. In the press box, John Dollins, a reporter from Waco, Texas, responded to a question regarding his betting interest, and, yes, he would stay loyal to his state. "We're trying to get pari-mutuel racing back in Texas," he added. "We have quarter-horse racing now. A quarter horse is anything that can outrun a calf."[4]

Jockeys riding in their first Derby are always a good "study," and Warren Mehrtens was no exception. Once on the track for the post parade, the twenty-five-year-old Brooklyn native looked like he had been born at Churchill Downs, he appeared calm; but inside he was churning like crazy.

"I was as nervous as a cat on Derby day. I was walking up and down; going to the bathroom all day long. I thought the race would never come," Mehrtens said about his pre-race nerves. One thing that bothered him was the position of their stall in the starting gate. The way the gate slanted, they had a near-straight run to the inside rail. "We were at such a slant," said Mehrtens, "that I was looking right at the rail and all I

Assault became a popular racehorse in the 1940s, not only for his Triple Crown heroics but also for his courage in overcoming numerous physical ailments during his career.

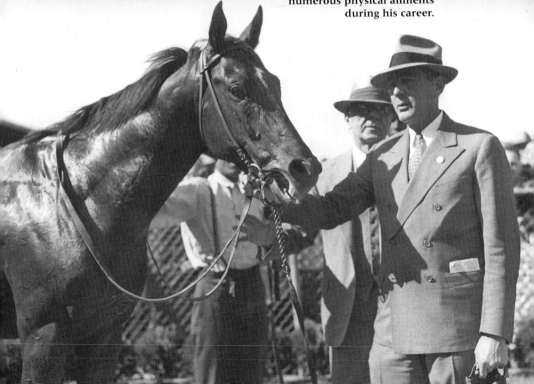

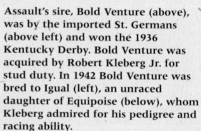

Assault's sire, Bold Venture (above), was by the imported St. Germans (above left) and won the 1936 Kentucky Derby. Bold Venture was acquired by Robert Kleberg Jr. for stud duty. In 1942 Bold Venture was bred to Igual (left), an unraced daughter of Equipoise (below), whom Kleberg admired for his pedigree and racing ability.

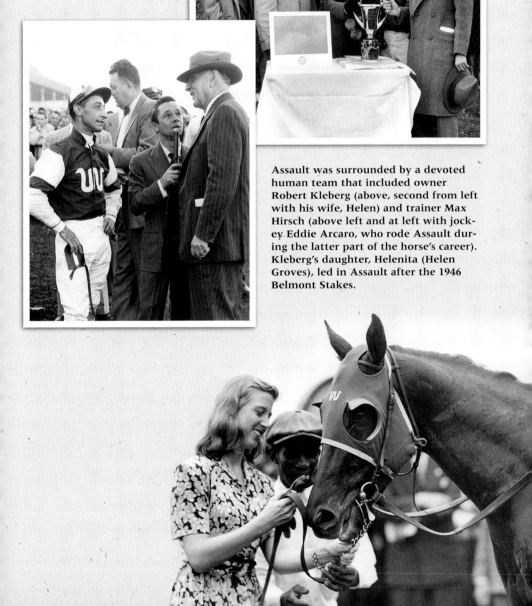

Assault was surrounded by a devoted human team that included owner Robert Kleberg (above, second from left with his wife, Helen) and trainer Max Hirsch (above left and at left with jockey Eddie Arcaro, who rode Assault during the latter part of the horse's career). Kleberg's daughter, Helenita (Helen Groves), led in Assault after the 1946 Belmont Stakes.

Assault's regular rider at two and three was Warren Mehrtens (above and below right). Arcaro (left) guided the colt to major victories at four. Dave Gorman (below left) rode Assault to the colt's last major victory in 1949.

As a foal, Assault severely injured his foot when he stepped on a surveyor's stake. The foot healed but had the appearance of a "clubfoot" (left) and caused Assault to trip or limp when he walked. But no trace of the injury showed when he ran, as he proved at three with easy victories in the Experimental Free Handicap No. 1 (above) and the Wood Memorial (top).

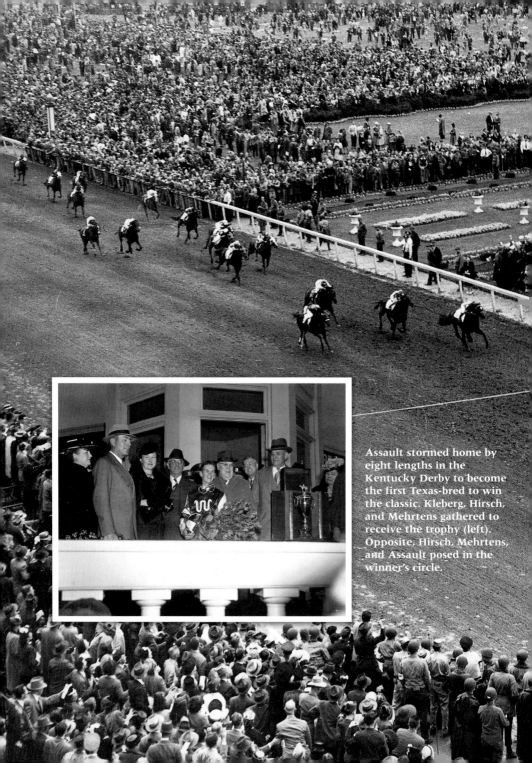

Assault stormed home by eight lengths in the Kentucky Derby to become the first Texas-bred to win the classic. Kleberg, Hirsch, and Mehrtens gathered to receive the trophy (left). Opposite, Hirsch, Mehrtens, and Assault posed in the winner's circle.

The Preakness proved more difficult, but Assault held off Lord Boswell to win by a neck (below). In the winner's circle Helenita Kleberg and a blanket of black-eyed Susans awaited him.

Assault captured the Belmont Stakes by three lengths (above) and returned to the winner's circle as racing's seventh Triple Crown winner.

Assault closed out his three-year-old campaign with easy victories in the Pimlico Special (below) and the Westchester Handicap (above). The 1946 Horse of the Year then received a well-deserved vacation.

At four Assault returned to win the Grey Lag Handicap (above), then followed with a victory in the Dixie Handicap (left), in which he was ridden for the first time by Arcaro. Kleberg, Alice Kleberg, and Arcaro accepted the Dixie trophy from A.G. Vanderbilt.

Assault notched his fifth straight victory in the Suburban (above), carrying 130 pounds for the first time. He repeated his performance in the Brooklyn (below), then made an electrifying rush to defeat Stymie in the Butler (top).

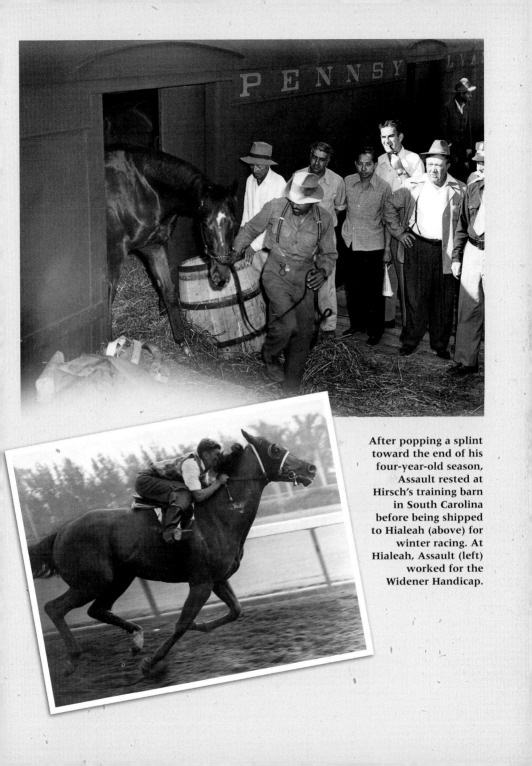

After popping a splint toward the end of his four-year-old season, Assault rested at Hirsch's training barn in South Carolina before being shipped to Hialeah (above) for winter racing. At Hialeah, Assault (left) worked for the Widener Handicap.

In his five-year-old debut Assault won an allowance race at Hialeah (below) but finished fifth in the Widener and came out of the race lame. He returned sixteen months later to capture the 1949 Brooklyn Handicap (above) for his last major victory. However, his final career win came in November 1950 at Hollywood Park (left) in a prep for the Hollywood Gold Cup.

After his final retirement Assault was returned to King Ranch (above, the main house and the range beyond). Virtually sterile, Assault never sired any Thoroughbred offspring. He was honored at King Ranch in an unusual way (below).

Assault lived out his days at King Ranch and was buried there after his death in 1971 at age twenty-eight.

could think about then was getting Assault to break well or else we would be in the back of the pack."[5]

Mehrtens hustled his colt out of there, avoiding the jam that materialized on the rail, then allowed Assault to settle on his own. Everyone expected Spy Song to make the early pace, and he did, leading Knockdown and Dark Jungle into the first turn. Assault was fifth after a half-mile.

The top three remained in those positions down the backstretch, while Assault found his path along the rail and moved into fourth after another quarter-mile had been run. By then, the ten-furlong horses were separating themselves from the wanna-bes. Only one runner was coming to the top as pure cream. On the far turn, Spy Song was running out of gas and drifted away from the rail. Mehrtens took the opportunity to lay his whalebone-handled whip across Assault's flanks. The little chestnut jetted through the opening at the top of the stretch like a spray of water squeezed through a chute and pulled away with every stride. Two lengths; three. Five lengths; six, seven.

Prior to 1946 only three winners had winning margins of eight lengths: Old Rosebud in 1914; Johnstown,

1939; and Whirlaway in 1941. And this time, the unlikeliest of winners, Assault. The greatest margin among the fifty-eight winners since has been Spend a Buck's five and a quarter lengths in 1985.

Assault's momentum carried him well into the backstretch, where a couple of outriders finally caught up with him and hauled him in. Mehrtens, still packaged at about one hundred pounds, was tired but ecstatic. The only downside to the colt's effort was the winning time — 2:06 3/5 for the ten furlongs. But it must be recalled that three days of unrelenting rain had left the track muddy all day until the Derby, when it was listed as slow.

So many thousands of people flowed onto the track that Kleberg wasn't able to reach the presentation stand in time to be interviewed on the radio hookup. But, for posterity, those close by heard him say that it had always been his desire to see a Texas-born and -raised horse win the Kentucky Derby. The question inevitably came up about Assault's breeding. Kleberg was only too happy to oblige. "Line-breeding to Commando is what makes Assault run in the stretch." Then he smiled. "I'm sorry the English don't have more of that in their stud book."[6] Unlike Kleberg, Max Hirsch had no trouble making it to the stand in time. Yes, the race went exactly as he expected. Did Warren Mehrtens feel the same way? "No, he didn't run like I expected — I didn't know he was going to run that fast."[7]

When the governor of the commonwealth of Kentucky, Simeon Willis, extended a hand to Hirsch, he said, "Mr. Hirsch, Kentucky salutes Texas for producing this great runner."

Hirsch gripped the hand firmly. "We always salute Kentucky."[8]

And what about the rest of the runners? There were the usual excuses: He didn't like the track. He was cut off in the stretch. Yet no one entertained the thought "my horse would have won if..." Johnny Longden, aboard Spy Song, mentioned the big opening he provided Assault when Spy Song tired and drifted out. "I could have made him go around, but he'd have won today no matter what any of us could have done." Hampden would have likely taken second had not his jockey Job Jessop misjudged the finish line and eased up on him too soon. But that was for second, far removed from Assault flying in front. Another rider complained about some crowding on the first turn, but regardless, "Assault was too much horse."[9]

The journalists were all of equal mind. From a Louisville newspaper the day after the race: "It wasn't Assault in the Kentucky Derby yesterday. It was murder! The way he ran away with the race in the stretch you'd have thought Assault was being chased by 16 cops.

"The Lone Star yesterday from the Lone Star State won by the width of Texas. As he flew away from them in the stretch, the only hope the other horses seemed to have of ever catching Assault was to hang around when the race was over and wait for him to revisit the scene of his crime."

The owner of the Waldorf Astoria in Louisville stood before his friends in his suite, a much less boisterous group. The owner himself was a little red-faced. The morning newspaper lay in scattered sections across the sofa. The headline screamed:

"ASSAULT WINS BY EIGHT!"

And another: "IT WASN'T ASSAULT. IT WAS MURDER!"

"I know what I promised yesterday," he said apologetically. "But can you picture me, or one of you, asking someone to join you for a drink in the Assault Room?"

So while Assault's name was a headline writer's dream it didn't have quite the connotation of conviviality necessary for a bar in an upscale hotel.

"It was like Joe Louis beating Max Schmeling."

Assault, assuming he could have, didn't have time to dwell on having his name associated, for good or bad, with cocktail lounges. Only a week separated the Derby and Preakness in 1946, and on Sunday he boarded the train for Baltimore. Much had occurred in the half-century since Max Hirsch had arrived as a boy in Baltimore, hiding in a stock car, hungry and cold.

Meanwhile, the accolades continued for Assault's smashing win at Churchill Downs. Texans, especially, could barely contain themselves. Sid Feder of the Associated Press wrote that upon Assault's crossing the finish line, Texans in the crowd let out a collective "Yipee-yi-yay!" — so loud you could hear it like gunfire over the roar of the finish.

The little horse was developing quite a following, and in the Preakness he went off as the favorite for the first time in fourteen starts. But he still had his detractors who were convinced he wasn't as good as he looked in Louisville.

"The best of a poor lot," some said.

"He had one freakish race. Look at his times; that tells you something."

His slow times were troubling, indicating he wasn't beating anything. The Preakness should winnow out the chaff. Many horsemen consider it the toughest of the three to win. With the Preakness at a mile and three-sixteenths, the Derby horses must drop down a half-furlong from the Derby distance. Then there's the tighter-turns story, which many horsemen, and writers, shrug off as bunk. The Preakness usually includes new faces, horses that skipped the Derby to train specifically for the Preakness. The 1946 renewal was no different.

On form, the best of the new entries was Natchez, a smallish chestnut son of Jamestown, owned by Mrs. Walter M. Jeffords and trained by Oscar White, whose most notable recent success was 1945 Belmont winner Pavot. Lovemenow from Cedar Farm received some play and went off at less than 11-1, while Tidy Bid should have stayed in the barn.

Maine Chance Farm continued to shadow Assault, this time without Perfect Bahram. When the windows closed at post time, Maine Chance's entry of Lord Boswell and Knockdown went off as second choice at 2-1. Hampden, the Derby third-place finisher, was third choice at 3-1. Assault was favored at 1.40-1.

Jockey John Gilbert gunned Natchez from the gate and right into Assault. The bumping put the Texas colt well back early, but Mehrtens didn't panic and took Assault around the field nearing the bottom of the backstretch. So dominating was his move that Assault had four lengths on the field by the time they topped the turn into the stretch. The crowd, on its feet, yelled for more.

But a threat loomed in the form of Lord Boswell, bearing down on the leader in the stretch. Mehrtens had been so confident just moments before, although the thought struck him going down the backstretch that he may have erred. "I didn't want to be in front," he admitted after the race, "and I thought, 'Oh, my God. What do I do now?' " Mehrtens hit him then, but Assault ducked away from the blow. "So I hand rode him the rest of the way," he said, "...and Lord Boswell almost caught me."[1]

A record Preakness crowd of more than 44,000 cheered the Texas horse to a neck victory, a performance that gave his detractors fuel to justify their claim that he wasn't a top-class colt, including his time of 2:01 2/5, which was five seconds slower than Riverland's track record.

"I moved too soon," Mehrtens said in an effort to take criticism away from the colt, "and when I hit him once at the head of the stretch, he ducked...I was afraid that if I hit him anymore, he might sulk and back up, so I didn't hit him again. Maybe I hit him in the wrong place or he didn't expect it or something, but he ducked from it. I think he'd have won by farther if I hadn't hit him."

Max Hirsch totally agreed, especially looking back at Natchez's antics at the break. "Assault got slammed around all through the first eighth. The jockey had to make a lot of use of him to regain the lost ground, and maybe he got a little flustered and made too much use of him. Anyway, Assault had to run the whole race without drawing a deep breath. Sure he got tired in the stretch. Who wouldn't?"[2]

Hirsch wanted to make sure Assault had all the lung

capacity he needed for the grueling Belmont Stakes, and he decided to use the colt's own love of competition to ready him for the task.

In the ensuing three weeks Hirsch worked Assault twice at a mile and a half, both in relays with other horses. One barn mate would run with him for six furlongs before giving way to another. When Hirsch saddled him on June 1, Assault hummed with power. He seemed as tuned as a south Texas rattler ready to strike.

Hirsch may have had him a little too wound up, however.

When the gates opened for the Belmont Stakes, Assault's head dropped. As he fought to regain his footing, Mehrtens fought to stay in the saddle. His only saving grace that day and the only thing that kept hopes for a Triple Crown alive was that he was riding with longer stirrups, which Hirsch, through his long experience as a trainer, requested of his jockeys.

The official start showed him in seventh, but a good turn of foot put him in fourth and on the rail by the first turn. Five lengths separated him from Foxcatcher Farm's Hampden with Eddie Arcaro aboard at the half, and at the mile that distance had increased to eight lengths.

Assault began his move approaching the far turn, first disposing of War Watch, who was never a factor and quickly faded. He swung into the stretch where only Hampden and Natchez stood between him and glory. Meanwhile, fans looked for Lord Boswell, but it wasn't his day, and he would finish fifth.

In overtaking Hampden, Assault swerved just a bit and brushed Arcaro's mount, but he wouldn't be denied and drove well clear of Hampden and Natchez to win with authority by three.

A breathless Mehrtens afterward admitted the contact with Arcaro's horse and was sure Arcaro would file a protest. He didn't. "I saw Natchez in front," he said, "got Assault out running, and we won. I just wanted to ride a good race. I never thought the Triple Crown would happen to me."[3]

Was he ever worried during the race? "Coming out of the gate," Mehrtens admitted to author Jim Bolus in *Derby Magic*. "He recovered at once, and we were never in difficulty again. I had more confidence this time than in either the Derby or the Preakness, but I still can't believe we've won the Triple Crown."

Assault completed the distance respectably, running

the mile and a half in 2:30 4/5. Still his detractors continued their jabs, pointing to unworthy rivals, and even taking a jab at the Triple Crown. Assault's sweep was the third in the 1940s, thus far, following Whirlaway in 1941 and Count Fleet in 1943. It had become too easy.

But Assault had his champions. One was Haden Kirkpatrick, a top racing journalist of the day. "In the Belmont field he was the scrawniest looking animal of the lot. But obviously he is an individual who has his mind on his work, rather than on primping, because when the parade ended and the running started, he assumed permanent control of the situation," he wrote. As for his being the best of a poor lot, Kirkpatrick scoffed, "If his competitors seem bad, it's because he makes them look that way."

On the subject of the Triple Crown, no less than Eddie Arcaro got a bit testy in Assault's defense. "Winning the Triple Crown is hard to do. There are three different races, three different tracks, and three different distances. A lot of horses can win in a mile and a quarter, or a mile and three-sixteenths; but when you're talking about a mile and a half, you'd better be another breed of cat."[4]

Texans' reactions at home were what one would expect. A petition to proclaim a holiday for Assault was sent to Governor Coke Stevenson. Returning pari-mutuel wagering on horse racing to Texas picked up in earnest. The Texas legislature had repealed pari-mutuel wagering in 1937 after legalizing it just four years earlier.

Monte Moncrief was attending veterinary school at Texas A&M College then — it wouldn't become a university until years later. The future veterinarian for King Ranch said that everyone "knew about Assault. Just as Dallas is proud of the Cowboys, Texas was proud of Assault." He compared the colt's Triple Crown victory to Joe Louis' huge upset over boxing's world champion Max Schmeling.

Meanwhile, Assault revealed a taste for the simple things in life — chocolate cake. Hirsch's cook, Virgie Malin, baked a brown-and-white cake; King Ranch colors, of course. Assault relished it, and from then on he got one after every win.

Hirsch gave the colt little time to rest on his laurels. The fifty-eighth Dwyer Stakes, a stern test at ten furlongs, was in two weeks. Despite giving weight to his rivals on the scale, including five pounds to his old foe

Lord Boswell, Assault had an easy time of it, winning by four and a half lengths over E.P. Taylor's Windfields. Lord Boswell was third.

The Dwyer being his fourth straight win and sixth in his last seven starts on the year vaulted Assault's earnings to nearly $340,000. It was already more than Gallant Fox's former one-year earnings record of $308,275. But even his growing legion of fans knew that Assault would soon have to go outside his age division to continue being considered for Horse of the Year. The handicap division of 1946 was as good a bunch as ever had a bar of lead put in their saddle pads, a cast that included the likes of Pavot, Lucky Draw, the great mare Gallorette, and Calumet Farm's smasher Armed.

And then there was Stymie.

But first there was the task of going on with the schedule Max Hirsch had laid for Assault, the first being against his crop mates in the mile and a quarter Arlington Classic at Arlington Park on July 27. The race, with its winner's share of $76,850, was a "gimme" for Assault. None of the five opponents figured to give Assault any trouble.

That's why they run races.

The crowd's favorite at 7-10, and carrying top weight of 126 pounds, Assault was full of run, and Mehrtens had all he could handle when the colt tried to run up on the heels of another horse in the first turn. The Dude led the field down the backstretch and when Assault began reeling him in, the Triple Crown winner brushed with Sgt. Spence and Mighty Story, running just behind The Dude. The chart notes indicate that he "loafed thereafter." But everyone on hand saw him backing up in distress.

Max Hirsch was alarmed by the shape Assault was in by the time he reached the stall. Sweating profusely, the colt laid down for about fifteen minutes. The cause was eventually traced to his kidneys, possibly stones.

As badly as his fans hoped to see their old hero back, it was not to be, at least for about six weeks. The September 7 Discovery Handicap, a nine-furlong race for three-year-olds at Aqueduct, marked his return to competition. Carrying up to twenty-one pounds more than his eight rivals, Assault was taken too far back, according to critics and was unable to catch the leader to finish third. A week later he came from sixth, next to last, to pass the leader Mighty Story but couldn't hold off Mrs. Walter M. Jeffords' Mahout, who had closed from last. Assault finished second to him by a half-length.

While his fans wondered what was wrong, Assault prepared for one of the biggest races of his career — the September 25 Manhattan Handicap. At least, the race had special meaning for Max Hirsch. Assault would meet Stymie for the first time, and Hirsch desperately wanted to beat the older horse.

Hirsch himself would tell you that it was just a part of racing. You win some; you lose some. Still the subject of Stymie remained a festering sore to be scratched for a long time. Stymie was the big fish that got away from Hirsch.

Stymie was foaled on King Ranch on April 9, 1941. He had embodied Robert Kleberg's breeding ideal: Man o' War and Commando. The flaming-red colt had a double dose of the former. When Kleberg was still building his breeding operation, he purchased the stallion Equestrian, who was by the great racehorse Equipoise out of the Man o' War mare Frilette. In 1940 Equestrian was bred to Stop Watch, a black daughter of

On Watch—Sunset Gun, by Man o' War. It was from On Watch that Kleberg got the Domino blood he loved.

The blaze-faced Stymie was officially bred by Max Hirsch due to the tardiness with which The Jockey Club transferred Stop Watch's name from Hirsch to King Ranch. Hirsch wasn't very impressed with Stymie when he began training and entered him for a $2,500 price on May 7, 1943, at Jamaica. Stymie finished seventh of nine in that one and next to last in a field of twelve in his next out. So Hirsch dropped him into a $1,500 race at Belmont on June 2. Despite another dismal performance, Stymie caught the attention of a former pigeon racer named Hirsch Jacobs. The common denominator of both pigeons and horses is speed, and Hirsch Jacobs knew how to get it out of both. The leading trainer of races won from 1933 to 1939 and 1941 to 1944, Jacobs had a knack for turning claimers into stakes winners.

But Stymie wasn't an overnight success; in fact, he didn't break his maiden until his eleventh start for Jacobs' "boss" and wife, Ethel D. Jacobs. Fast forward to 1946. By that time, Stymie had garnered wins in the Saratoga Cup (twice), the Whitney, the Brooklyn

Handicap, the Pimlico Cup, plus the Grey Lag (twice), Butler, Westchester, and Edgemere handicaps. His earnings totaled nearly half a million dollars, and he was one of the most popular runners in the country.

For Max Hirsch, Stymie's success was salt in the wound.

In the Manhattan Handicap at Belmont, Assault was stepping out of his division for the first time, necessary if he wanted to stay in the running for the Horse of the Year title. But he first had to beat Stymie. Assault was improving but still wasn't running with the same old confidence. Now he was going to need that old arrogance like never before.

Warren Mehrtens was hardly the picture of confidence himself as he was legged up on Assault and rode him to the track for the mile and a half race. He avoided eye contact with reporters, smiled weakly at the fans calling for Assault. The colt was the only three-year-old in the field of eight. He carried 116 pounds, while Pavot, with Eddie Arcaro on board, had 121. The high weight with 126 pounds was Stymie, with Basil James up. The fans backed Assault at the windows but sent Stymie off even lower. If Assault was a fan

favorite, Stymie was an icon. The copper-colored King Ranch castoff played his role in every way.

He normally started his runs from about mid-pack, or even farther back. Sometimes those who held tickets on him tore them up in frustration. But wherever he was on the track, Stymie signaled his intentions to start a drive by raising his head. When the head came up, the crowd roared, "Here comes Stymie!"

In the Manhattan Stymie raised his head shortly after going a mile, moved into second place with a quarter-mile to go, and outdueled Pavot for the win. Assault was too far back to catch the top two and dead-heated for third with Flareback. Hirsch couldn't help but be disappointed.

When Assault was beaten by the three-year-old filly Bridal Flower (who would later become his stable-mate) in the October 19 Roamer Handicap at Jamaica, the fans began muttering. Even Hirsch had to stifle his growing frustration. Warren Mehrtens avoided him when he could, but there would be no avoiding the trainer after the Gallant Fox Handicap on October 26.

The field for the mile and five-eighths race was a classy one that included Stymie, Pavot, the

Argentinian champion filly Miss Grillo, and George Widener's five-year-old Lucky Draw. Assault, under 114 pounds, and Risolater, carrying only 108, were the only three-year-olds. A gelded bay son of Jack High, Lucky Draw had won five races in a row, four in track-record time, and defeated the likes of Stymie, Gallorette, Armed, and Pavot. The high weight at 129 pounds, he went off as the odds-on favorite with Assault the second choice at 4-1 and Stymie at 5-1. Pavot was at 7-1.

For the race, the media created a new angle — an in-state rivalry between the two Texas-breds. The publicity was good for racing and especially good for Texas.

Eleven horses started, and after running a half-mile Stymie had only a 68-1 longshot beaten. Meanwhile, Warren Mehrtens had a snug hold on Assault, letting him run in the front group, while Lucky Draw briefly traded the lead with the 74-1 longshot Speeding Home, who quickly retreated. After another two quarters, Stymie had moved only to eighth with Assault picking up steam and taking over third. Then, two things happened: Assault inherited the lead from a spent Lucky Draw and Stymie's head came up. The

crowd at old Jamaica rose as one, their voices building to an unearthly noise.

Two furlongs farther, Stymie's drive was relentless and had carried him into second place, one length behind Assault. Coming fastest of all was the South American Rico Monte, and Assault wilted under the double-barreled attack. Stymie swept past him and moved out to lead by five. Rico Monte, too, had Assault beaten and at the wire had cut Stymie's advantage in half, forcing the son of Equestrian to a track-record of 2:42 4/5. Assault finished another two lengths behind Rico Monte but eight lengths ahead of fourth-place finisher Miss Grillo. Bounding Home, Pavot, and Lucky Draw were all farther back.

While the race was a good one for Assault, Hirsch felt Mehrtens had moved too soon on the colt, not leaving enough in the stretch against the top two. And the loss was Assault's sixth straight, two of them to Stymie. Hirsch firmly believed Stymie wasn't a better racehorse. In fact, he was convinced that Assault could beat him anywhere, any time, and at any distance. To do it would take the coolest of heads and an unwavering discipline. In the 1940s that meant Eddie Arcaro.

It also meant taking Warren Mehrtens off the colt, and although Hirsch had Kleberg's blessing, he did not relish delivering the news. He remembered the kid who showed up at his Belmont barn looking for a job. Warren had been a star high diver on the Jamaica High School swimming team in New York and was even Olympic material, but he told Hirsch he wanted to ride horses.

Hirsch would later say that Mehrtens had "lost confidence in the horse. He thought Assault didn't have it any more — and was afraid to wait with him and make his move as I told him to. He was running him up there too soon and taking too much out of him. 'Flesh and bone can stand only so much,' I told him. 'You're asking too much of the horse.' "[5]

So before giving Arcaro the leg up for the November 1 Pimlico Special, Hirsch told him in no uncertain terms how he wanted the race run: "This horse can beat Stymie at any distance. A mile...two miles...four miles. Never mind those other horses in the race. You watch Stymie. When James (Basil, Stymie's jockey) makes his move, you move with him. Stymie will outrun you for an eighth of mile, maybe, but no more. After that, he's yours."[6]

An electric current ran through the Pimlico crowd. Whether one was a fan of Stymie's or Assault's, the feeling was that this was going to be the day, the place, and the time.

Only four went to the post — the big two as well as the outstanding filly Bridal Flower and the solid handicapper Turbine. Stymie was the overwhelming favorite in the $25,000 winner-take-all event; his odds, 70 cents on the dollar. Assault was bet down to just under 3-1, and Bridal Flower, who hadn't raced since beating Assault in the Roamer, was at 4-1. Turbine, not surprisingly, was the longshot at 11-1.

The filly went straight to the front, stalked by Turbine. Surprising was how far behind Assault and Stymie lagged at the half, posted in :48 1/5. Assault was fourteen lengths off of Bridal Flower's pace and Stymie was another four back. In another quarter, the distance from the front had decreased to nine and a half lengths, while Assault added three to his advantage over Stymie.

Then Stymie raised his head. The roar from the crowd told Arcaro that he was coming. He sat chilly on Assault and waited, recalling his questioning Max

Hirsch why he would replace Mehrtens, and that Hirsch had replied that there was one reason: Arcaro could manage Assault better.

Did Arcaro think Assault was better than Stymie? He'd soon find out. After a mile, Assault and Stymie had closed the gap on the leaders. At about the quarter pole Stymie drew even to Assault's saddle. Arcaro waited for an imminent opening on the rail and turned his mount loose. Assault responded, and the question of superiority was answered. With Stymie still hanging on to his saddlecloth, Assault took the lead from Bridal Flower and moved out to a length lead, then two lengths, then four. He won by six in 1:57, just three-fifths off Riverland's track record of 1:56 2/5 for the mile and three-sixteenths.

Lest anyone believe Assault wasn't back, he closed his season eight days later at Jamaica in the Westchester Handicap, also run at a mile and three-six-teenths. Stymie was absent, but nearly 39,000 watched Assault whip Lucky Draw and the top handicap mare Gallorette in 1:56 2/5, one and a fifth second off Lucky Draw's track record set that July.

On the basis of his wins in the classics and beating

Stymie and Gallorette later, Assault was voted Horse of the Year and the champion in his age bracket for 1946. He would be even better the next year, although circumstances beyond his control would also lend a controversy to his career that he would never live down.

ASSAULT

CHAPTER 8

"Heart of a lion"

Thoroughbreds are supposed to grow from boys into men during their transition from three to four. Assault may not have blossomed into a "hunk" of a horse, but Joe Palmer wrote in *American Race Horses of 1947* of his growing "from a rather plain but substantial three-year-old into a very handsome four-year-old." The chestnut colt was measured in August and found to stand 15.1 hands at the withers. Hirsch estimated that Assault weighed 975 pounds; Kleberg, 1,050 pounds.

"This pictures a small, but very well developed horse," Palmer continued. Interestingly, Palmer also wrote of Assault's change in personality, which he said had "developed more than his body." A "matter-of-fact kind of colt" early in his three-year-old season, Assault soon discovered he was "head of the stable and over the winter he became even more certain."

Although Assault was never mean, he was allowed some latitudes that no one else would have enjoyed. He once caused the entire stable to be fed early because he spied his feed tub outside his stall fifteen minutes before feeding time. Hirsch believed in giving a horse all he wanted to eat, but of Assault's appetite he told Palmer, "I know that no horse can digest as much as Assault wants to eat. He's perpetually hungry."

As for his foot, it was never normal and never would be. After being pared down early in the winter, the foot grew back as close to normal as could be expected. Like all the Hirsch horses, Assault was exercised barefoot during the winter. When he was first shod on March 1, the foot was better than when Hirsch initially saw it. Still, John Dern would always have his work cut out for him.

Assault debuted as a four-year-old on May 3, the day before the anniversary of his Kentucky Derby win. It was fitting that the beginning of his handicap season be in a race named for a grand handicap horse Max Hirsch had trained and valued so highly — Grey Lag.

Hirsch had Assault dead fit for the opener, in which he was assigned top weight of 128 pounds with 126 on Stymie. These two were the real class in the field, but

Coincidence and Lets Dance were both capable runners and getting eight and eighteen pounds, respectively. Stymie's performance was disappointing
although his fans could point to anything but a smooth
trip. Assault didn't have the smoothest of trips either.
Coming into the stretch, Lets Dance bumped him and
carried him wide. Warren Mehrtens, who was back
aboard Assault, didn't panic, and urged him onward
until the leaders had been run down to win by a neck
over Lets Dance. Coincidence was another neck back
with Stymie two lengths back in fourth. Assault's time
for the nine furlongs was officially listed as 1:49 4/5,
one-fifth of a second off Jamaica's standard. But a *Daily
Racing Form* clocker stopped him in 1:49 1/5. All in all,
it was an outstanding showing for a first out, and it was
just a beginning.

With an additional pound of lead and Arcaro back in
the saddle, Assault added another impressive effort six
days later in the Dixie Handicap at Pimlico. Rico Monte,
the speedster from Argentina, gave Assault a fight but
lost to him by a half-length. Assault crossed the wire in
time of 1:57 4/5 for the mile and three-sixteenths.

One of the biggest races for the handicap year

promised another showdown with Stymie with Arcaro again in the saddle on Assault. The sixty-first running of the mile and a quarter Suburban Handicap included in the seven-horse field, besides the top two, Assault's old rival from the classics, Natchez, as well as Rico Monte. Assault carried 130 pounds, giving four to Stymie, ten to Natchez, and eleven to Rico Monte.

Stymie's legion felt redemption close at hand, insisting that he got the worst of the interference in the Grey Lag. Assault's backers pointed out that Stymie didn't make up any lost ground in the final sixteenth. Despite his impost and the concessions to some pretty fair runners, Assault went off a strong favorite ($1.10) with Stymie at nearly 2-1.

There would be no redemption today for Stymie fans. Running fifth, the copper-colored colt coasted along about four lengths behind Assault, who was fourth in the early going while Natchez played "catch me" on an early and comfortable lead. Stymie had no excuse and flattened out in the stretch to finish fourth. Assault handled beautifully for Arcaro and caught Natchez near the finish to draw off by two lengths. It was another eight lengths back to Stymie. Assault completed the mile and a quarter in 2:01 4/5 on a fast track. His connections pocketed $40,100, which was significant money.

The June 21 Brooklyn Handicap at Aqueduct gave Stymie supporters new hopes. For one, Assault picked up three pounds and Stymie dropped two. Gallorette's scratch left five in the field, but there were only two as far as the bettors and really interested parties were concerned. But just for record's sake, the three starters completing the field were Larky Day, Concordian, and Windfields, the three getting from nineteen to twenty-four pounds from the top-weighted Texan.

E.P. Taylor's Windfields took an early lead and carried it to a margin of three to four lengths to deep stretch. Assault gave his backers a scare when he stumbled at the start. Stymie broke more alertly then settled at the rear of the field. After a half-mile, fifteen lengths separated him from the lead; after six furlongs, thirteen lengths. Arcaro, in the meantime, placed Assault where he was supposed to and kept Stymie in his rearview mirror. After a mile, which Windfields covered in a leisurely 1:38, the King Ranch colt was five and a half lengths off the pace, with four on Stymie, and beginning to roll.

Very soon Stymie began his offense. But Assault was ahead of him, a length and half in the stretch call and three lengths easily at the wire. It was a smashing performance. Moreover, the $38,100 winner's purse vaulted him to the top of the world's money earners with $576,670.

Then Hirsch put Assault in the stall for a three-week breather. His next scheduled start was the Butler Handicap at Jamaica on July 12. Hirsch Jacobs, on the other hand, sent Stymie out to win the June 28 Questionnaire Handicap and the July 5 Sussex Handicap. The combined purses of $39,075 gave him career earnings of $595,510. He would hold the leading money-earners title barely longer than had Assault.

The Butler, like the Brooklyn, was only a field of five. The Argentinian Rico Monte was back, but he had had too many battles against Assault. His tank would run empty. The speed, if there were any in the race, would come from the four-year-old Risolater. Rico Monte and Risolater carried 121 pounds and 111 pounds, respectively.

Jamaica racing secretary John B. Campbell assigned Assault his heaviest impost to date, 135 pounds, and Stymie, 126 pounds.

The last of the top three was the great mare
Gallorette, with 117 pounds. Any doubt she belonged
in a field like this could be dispelled by a look at her
record. The previous year she had won the Brooklyn
and Metropolitan over the boys, as well as the Beldame
in her own division to earn champion older mare honors. She was big and rugged and could give right back
what she got. In a mid-century poll (1950) of the greatest mares, she was number one.

The day was bright and sunny and a crowd of
32,395 came out to back Assault down to odds-on at
forty-five cents to the dollar. Stymie was the second
choice at nearly 3-1 and Gallorette was at 9-1.

No one really wanted to go to the front, but
Risolater, starting in the number one post position,
came out first; Rico Monte, second. As for the top
three, Gallorette lay in third, four lengths ahead of
Assault with Stymie another three lengths back after a
half-mile in :49 for the mile and three-sixteenths race.
Nothing changed in their positions for another quarter.
But like distant thunder heralding a summer storm,
the crowd sensed something about to break loose.

It happened on the far turn, the large end of the

egg-shaped Jamaica course, when Arcaro decided to move ahead on Assault. His aim was to move between Gallorette and Rico Monte, but Eric Guerin, riding W.L. Brann's great mare, moved with Gallorette, and she outran Assault for a sixteenth, causing Arcaro to take his colt back. He was beginning to wonder if he had made a huge mistake in not waiting for Stymie. But just then, Stymie moved.

Curving off the turn into the stretch, Gallorette joined Risolater and Rico Monte on the front end and then went on out to get a clear shot at the finish line. Stymie was going faster than anyone and surged ahead of Assault by about a half-length. Those two circled Gallorette, and Assault found himself wedged in the middle, "rather definitely committed to his course but without room to get through."[1]

The worst part came when the whip of Stymie's rider, Bobby Permane, arced across Assault and hit him at least three times, leaving marks. At this point only a furlong remained, and Arcaro had no place to go. Something had to break.

It was Gallorette. Running the race of her life, the mare finally began to fall back, and the vise holding

Assault loosened. Fewer than seventy yards remained.

The trip down the Jamaica stretch, as short as it is, might have seemed in slow motion for Arcaro, Permane, and Guerin. But from a spectator's perspective, even one as experienced as Joe Palmer's, the action ripped out in mind-boggling rapidity. He couldn't believe it when Assault made the move that put him even with his rivals.

"I was looking squarely at the performance with a pair of nine-power glasses, and I still don't know how he did it," wrote Palmer in *The Blood-Horse*.

After Gallorette broke up the troika, the race came down to whether Assault could pull it off. No one thought he could. But, in a finish that had to be seen to be believed, Assault surged past Stymie and the fading mare to beat his fellow Texan by a head. The din that arose from race-goers that day was more likely to have come from an F5 tornado than the throats of more than 32,000 spectators.

Assault's time, 1:56 3/5, was the fastest time for one and three-sixteenths miles run at Jamaica that season, and the $36,700 boosted his earnings to the top of the world with $613,370, making him the first horse to top

$600,000 in earnings. (Stymie also topped $600,000 with the $10,000 second-place money.) In addition, no other winner of the Butler had ever carried such a burden, the closest being the great Discovery with 132 pounds. Two years earlier a four-year-old Stymie won with just 121.

The Butler Handicap defined Assault. Wrote Joe Palmer in *The Blood-Horse*:

"My own opinion of Assault was high going into the race, but it is considerably higher now than if he had simply run down his field with clear sailing. It gave him a chance to show more heart than he has ever shown before and we wouldn't have known quite how great a horse he is if he hadn't been forced to do it the hard way."

Just a week after his Butler heroics, Belmont patrons installed him as odds-on favorite at fifty-five cents to the dollar for the premier running of the International Gold Cup. Stymie just missed going off the second choice with the three-year-old star Phalanx from the C.V. Whitney stable taking that honor at 4.60-1 and Stymie right behind at 4.75-1. All carried 126 pounds except Phalanx, who had an impost of 112 pounds.

Not many horses could have faced such a field at

equal weights over a mile and five-eighths, which just happened to be Stymie's best distance, and won only a week after such a heroic effort in the Butler. Neither could Assault. In the final sixteenth Assault swerved and then faltered under Stymie's withering rush. The latter won by a neck over Natchez, Assault's old rival from the previous year, with Assault another four lengths back. Stymie collected $73,000, which gave him an earnings title that looked to be safe for some time.

There were calls to retire Assault, that he had done enough to prove he was a great horse. And his body seemed to be wearing out. But he had one more race to run — the toughest kind of race — a match against Calumet Farm's champion gelding Armed. The idea for the match race came about because Armed was a gelding and not eligible for the Butler and also it would provide a showdown with Assault.

The race was scheduled for August 30 at Arlington Park. Benjamin Lindheimer, executive director at Arlington and Washington parks, knew such a race would generate a lot of interest, and Washington Park offered a $100,000 purse. Both Calumet and Robert Kleberg agreed to the terms — the race would be run at a mile and a quarter — considered to be the best distance for both horses.

Armed had enjoyed another of his marvelously consistent seasons. Prior to the match race he'd run fourteen times, won nine, and been second in four others. Included in his 1947 wins were track-record victories in the Gulfstream and Stars and Stripes handicaps, and the Whirlaway Stakes.

In the week leading up to the Arlington match race, Assault's regular exercise rider Pie Garcia was not available for the final work, and the colt, who had developed the bad habit of running off with his riders, took advantage of a new boy and away he went. During his moment of abandon, he severely strained himself and pulled up lame.

When Assault injured himself the match race was called off. He was returned to New York and healed rather quickly. Match race talk was revived. George D. Widener, president of the Westchester Racing Association, New York racing's governing body, offered to hold the race at Belmont Park, same distance and conditions as before. A date was set for Saturday, September 27.

Calumet and King Ranch were pleased; Hirsch Jacobs was not. And he commented vociferously about Stymie's being snubbed. It was a complicated mess, explained in the 1948 *American Racing Manual* that the Belmont race was the same race as had been planned for Chicago. Stymie's connections had not been willing to come to the Windy City because he was a poor shipper who did most of his racing around New York.

A few days before the race, Assault was said to be training badly again. The race, according to a September 23 *Louisville Chronicle* story, "became doubtful tonight when it was learned that trainer Max Hirsch was not satisfied that Assault would be at his peak for the mile and a quarter special." Hirsch said that Assault had not worked badly, but not as he had expected.

Two days later on Thursday, September 25, however, Assault was caught in 1:41 3/5 for a mile in the rain looking much better than he had in a while. But he came up lame afterwards. The problem showed up after he'd walked the shed row for a while, and it appeared to be a splint, a bony growth about two inches below the left knee, inside the cannon bone. "He was in real pain, but later he seemed to get better, and

118

finally he was walking almost all right," Hirsch said.

When reporters asked Hirsch about the race, he replied he would just have to see on Friday.

Hirsch stood opposite Robert Kleberg on running Assault in the match race. In fact, Kleberg had traveled to Belmont on Friday and examined his colt in the presence of Hirsch and a veterinarian. Hirsch, though, twice had commented he didn't want Assault to run because he was not in peak condition.

Kleberg told the *Lexington Leader* he probably wouldn't start Assault in "an ordinary stake race...but in a special race of this kind, where there would be no race if we scratched, we have decided to run...We hope that Assault will run as well as he worked Thursday."

Meanwhile, Belmont Park requested permission from the state racing commission to hold the race without pari-mutuel wagering due to Assault's condition, a request that chairman Ashley T. Cole not only granted but lauded. "Their action," he stated, "is in accordance with the highest traditions of the sport, and I hope that the public will so appreciate it."

Not everyone appreciated these turn of events, especially the news media. What had been called the

"Race of the Century" wrote Frank Ortell in the New York *World-Telegram*, was now a spectacle. "Innocent victims, of course, are Warren G. Wright, owner of Armed, and the horse's trainers, Ben and Jimmy Jones. They have everything to lose and nothing to gain. If Armed should win, with Assault collapsing, there will be little glory. If Assault should win, there will be jeers that Armed could not even beat an unsound horse."

As for the Jones boys, when Hirsch showed them Assault's lameness problem, they weren't impressed. There's probably some soreness, they agreed, but nothing serious.

With some 50,000 fans expected, Saturday's card was as classy as a day of racing comes. In addition to the match race, the sixth race of the day, Stymie would head the Manhattan Handicap, and Bewitch, another star from Calumet who was unbeaten in eight starts, topped the Matron.

The match race controversy continued throughout Friday and into Saturday. Most of the commentary roasted Max Hirsch, and even Assault was criticized for events over which he, of course, had no control. William Boniface, journalist for the *Baltimore Sun*, had difficulty finding anyone outside the state of Texas who would give Assault a snowball's chance of winning. To hear anything positive, he chatted with Eddie Arcaro in jockey's room.

"I still have a lot of confidence in Assault," the nation's money-leading rider said. "I've got to have, because he has carried me to some of the best wins of my career."

Doug Dodson, Armed's jockey, was just as sure of his chances. "I think we will win the match, but I have respect for Assault, and I'm sure Arcaro has the same for my horse. He oughta 'cause he's ridden him," Dodson told Boniface.

The combatants' records stood as follows:

Armed — Age 6. 54 starts, 33 wins, 13 seconds, 2 thirds, $642,900.

Assault — Age 4. 30 starts, 15 wins, 4 seconds, 5 thirds, $623,370.

Both owners agreed the winnings would go to charity, which did nothing to soothe ruffled feathers. In fact the 51,573 fans couldn't work up much enthusiasm for the exhibition the "Race of the Century" had turned into.

In the warm-up, fans cheered as Assault looked to

be jogging soundly. With an empty starting stall separating them, Assault and Armed broke at 4:16 p.m.
Eastern Time. The unofficial odds were 1-3 on
Calumet's gelding and 6-5 on the Texan. Armed quickly moved away from Assault. At the half-mile pole,
Assault began a move that carried him to within a
length and a half or two of his rival. This encouraging
move lasted to the three-eighths marker when Assault
dropped back quickly. Armed lengthened his lead.
With defeat imminent, Arcaro eased his mount.

Armed's followers cheered, but even their joy seemed
muted. Everyone knew as soon as Armed crossed the
line eight lengths ahead of his rival that his race would
become as controversial as Man o' War's drubbing by a
like margin of Sir Barton in their 1920 meeting. Sir
Barton, his shelly, brittle hooves compromised by
Kenilworth Park's unyielding surface, was only a spectre
of the galloper who was the first to win the Triple Crown.

Some journalists were almost disdainful in their
post-race remarks regarding Assault. One wrote that
he finished "sound." Joe Palmer was compelled to go
to Hirsch's stable to see for himself. He discovered that
"Assault had a big splint, about an inch and a half long,

some two inches under the left knee on the inside of the cannon. It had been there for most of the colt's life, but it apparently had worsened so it now involved the tendon. The writer pressed directly on the splint and Assault paid no attention. He (Palmer) pressed between the cannon and the tendon, and Assault took his foot away in a hurry. There was pain."[2]

Kleberg was furious at himself. He seemed to realize that when he overrode his trainer's decision not to start both in Chicago and in New York, he had painted himself into a corner. He had wanted the race.

"I got myself into this," Kleberg said angrily, "because I didn't realize what it would be like. Nobody will ever get me in a fix like this again. If I ever get in another match, there'll be a forfeit."[3]

Arcaro, who had a firsthand perspective of how the horse felt and who was never one to mince words, said Assault shouldn't have been run. "The poor guy, he was all heart. He wanted to go hard. But I didn't let him. You don't do that to someone you respect."[4]

Hirsch was angrier. Later, at the barn, Hirsch watched while William Daniels, Hirsch's stable foreman of some thirty-three years, and two handlers named Blackjack and Patsy de Coco applied a medicated bandage to Assault's bad leg. "Walk him a little," Hirsch ordered.

Patsy led the colt out of the stall and walked him around the shed row. Racing journalist Haden Kirkpatrick was on hand and wrote in *The Thoroughbred Record* that Assault looked "very sore." Hirsch was still upset. "Never should have run him," he told Kirkpatrick. "It just isn't right to start a horse in that condition. He's got a heart like a lion.

"By gosh he's game as they come though...It's a shame to get this kind of horse beat that way."

His anger mellowed as he talked about the splint. "It's funny but he's had it all his life. The thing never gave him a bit of trouble, though, until just a few days ago. It's right on the sheath of the tendon, and every step he takes must be just like thumping a boil.

"He's never had the best of it any time in his life. Always something to handicap him, but this is just too much, even for him.

"There never was another horse like him."

Despite his marvelous seven-race win streak, five if you count only those in 1947, during which he carried top weight and beat some classy runners, including Stymie, Assault lost out in the year-end polls to Armed for both champion handicap horse and Horse of the Year. Just two votes were cast for Assault, one for Stymie.

It had been planned to retire him after this race. But Kleberg and Hirsch thought if pinfiring (caustic treatment of the shin bone to stimulate circulation and tissue growth) the splint was successful, there was no reason he couldn't return in 1948. So the leg was pinfired, and he was shipped to Columbia, South Carolina, to rest and recover.

CHAPTER 9

Try, Try Again

A s 1948 dawned, Assault was giving Max Hirsch plenty to be pleased about. The splint that sent the horse to the sidelines the previous fall had healed completely, and Hirsch had begun prepping him for the February 21 Widener Handicap at Hialeah and a possible meeting with old rival Armed.

Assault, now five years old, was in training with other King Ranch horses at the Buxton Training Stables at the South Carolina state fairgrounds in Columbia. His stablemates included the outstanding filly But Why Not, who had earned champion three-year-old filly and handicap female honors the previous year, and Better Self, a top two-year-old in 1947 who had the misfortune to run into a colt named Citation.

As Assault continued his preparations for the Widener, Hirsch liked what he saw.

"If he continues to train all right, as he has been doing, he'll be in top shape to fulfill all his engagements," Hirsch told reporters that January.

Assault's first engagement was a seven-furlong allowance event at Hialeah on February 14. Only three others showed up, and Assault went off as the heavy favorite, but Rampart, a lightweight at 109 pounds to Assault's 128, gave the champion all he could handle. Rampart led almost from the start, while Assault was unhurried early. Warren Mehrtens was aboard again and rode a cool race, letting Assault pick his moment of attack. But Rampart didn't give way easily, forcing Assault to catch him near the wire for a head victory. Even with the close finish, the race proved Assault was fully recovered and raring to go with the Widener just a week away. And it was a message sent loud and clear to Calumet Farm. Armed also was scheduled to start in the Widener. However, the result wouldn't be what the connections of either horse expected.

Nine runners lined up for the mile and a quarter Widener. Assault and Armed each carried 130 pounds, giving from seventeen to twenty-seven pounds to the rest of the field. Assault, with Eddie Arcaro up, was the slight favorite over Armed at almost even money. Only two other horses had odds lower than double-digits: Incline and Riskolater, both at 9-1.

Armed was the old man of this year's Widener. At seven, he was not the same runner he had been the previous two years when he won twenty-two of thirty-five outings, including the previous two runnings of the Widener. He had already started five times in 1948, with only one win, a six-furlong allowance, to show for it. He came into the Widener off a third-place finish to longshot El Mono in the McLennan, the traditional Widener prep, run the week before. In fact, Assault was the only Widener runner who didn't compete in the McLennan. On February 18, just three days before the Widener, Assault had his final serious prep for the race, working ten furlongs in impressive style, going in 2:04 2/5.

As in his allowance prep the week before, Assault was taken back early in the Widener and allowed to settle. Armed was running mid-pack, while 50-1 shot Stud Poker set a lively pace — six furlongs in 1:11, a mile in 1:35 4/5 — followed by Lets Dance and Bug Juice. Down the backstretch Assault moved up on the outside of Armed, then challenged around the turn, closing to within a length and a half of Stud Poker with a quarter-mile to go. Armed, meanwhile, made only a mild rally and never threatened for the lead.

In the final furlong the four-year-old Head Play colt El Mono came flying from behind to just get past Stud Poker at the wire. Bug Juice, a nearly 60-1 shot, held on for third, while Assault faltered late and finished fifth after being passed by Armed in the stretch. Neither champion had performed up to expectations. In fact, the 15-1 shot El Mono broke Armed's track record of 2:01 3/5, set in the previous year's Widener, by three-fifths of a second.

For Robert Kleberg and Max Hirsch, the Widener was disheartening not so much because of where Assault finished but why he finished so poorly. He came out of the race sore, and Hirsch soon discovered the horse had popped a new splint as well as an osselet, a bony growth, on his left ankle — his good foot. The osselet probably resulted from years of compensating for his damaged right foot. Assault was immediately returned to Columbia and from there would be sent to King Ranch's Kentucky property, which had been part of the late E.R. Bradley's Idle Hour Farm near Lexington.

Assault's racing career finally appeared to be over. Since he had first stumbled in a post parade at two, he had accumulated thirty-three starts, sixteen victories, and ten placings, with earnings of $626,620.

Kleberg set Assault's stud fee at $2,500 and planned to breed a select group of mares to the stallion for the 1948 breeding season, including Stymie's dam Stop Watch (by On Watch), Coaching Club American Oaks winner Too Timely (Discovery), Better Self's dam Bee Mac (War Admiral), By Jimminy's dam Buginarug (Blue Larkspur), champion Bridal Flower (Challenger II), Selima Stakes winner Split Second (Sortie), and But Why Not's dam Be Like Mom (Sickle). Assault received good attention from outside breeders with his book quickly filling. In mid-March, the Darby Dan Farm mare Darby Damozel (by War Admiral) became the first mare to be bred to Assault.

No one associated with Assault was expecting the results a routine lab test produced, and why would they? All systems were go as far as the new stallion was concerned. But as a matter of course, a semen sample was sent to a local veterinary clinic for evaluation. The result was dismaying and a follow-up test was conducted. The result was the same. Respected veterinarian Charles Hagyard reported to J. Howard Rouse, the King Ranch Kentucky farm manager, that less than 1 percent of Assault's sperm cells were alive.

Rouse immediately contacted Kleberg, who instructed that Assault be pulled from stud duty and to cancel all bookings. Darby Damozel and one other mare had been bred to him before the tests, and, of course, neither mare was found to be in foal. The King Ranch mares that were scheduled to be bred to him were sent to other stallions. Kleberg was beyond disappointed. Assault's breeding; his winning the classics; beating Stymie; his courage — all of it in the genes. All of it for naught.

Assault was soon shipped to Texas, where he was allowed to "run out," and underwent fertility treatment at the ranch. By November, Assault was showing increasing numbers of live sperm cells; however, with all the rest he had gotten, he was sound again and galloping without lameness, and Kleberg toyed with the idea of racing the old warrior once more.

By January 1949, reports surfaced that Max Hirsch was putting Assault back into training and that the six-year-old would be getting into shape on a new training track at King Ranch instead of at Hirsch's South Carolina winter quarters.

"He never looked better — in fact, he never looked as good," Hirsch told a reporter with the *Lexington Herald*.

Hirsch didn't rush Assault, bringing him along slowly in the warm south Texas weather. By April the Texas comet was at Belmont Park, back in Hirsch's barn along with the rest of the King Ranch string. One of the Texas contingent was a boldly marked two-year-old son of Bold Venture named Middleground. Out of the Chicaro mare Verguenza, Middleground would win four of five starts that season, including the Hopeful Stakes, with his only non-win being a third in the Arlington Futurity.

Hirsch became impressed with the way Assault was coming along, and by early summer the little chestnut horse was deemed ready for a test. Hirsch chose a seven-furlong allowance at Aqueduct on June 24. It had been almost a year and a half since Assault had last seen competition, but he hadn't forgotten what to do.

Assault was ridden by Bill Boland, a young apprentice rider who the following year would ride Middleground to victory in the Kentucky Derby. Even with the apprentice rider's weight allowance, Assault still carried top weight, but 119 pounds was a far cry from the 135 pounds he had carried to victory in the Butler Handicap almost two years earlier. Five starters went to the post, and the crowd sent Assault to the gate their choice at odds-on.

Assault looked good and seemed in command when he took the lead at the top of the stretch. Boland, a sixteen-year-old Texas native, hand rode the old champion down the stretch, but he didn't count on longshot Michigan III's late charge. A recent import from Argentina, Michigan III, who was making his U.S. debut, got his nose in front at the wire for the upset.

While some racing pundits proclaimed that Boland was overconfident in his ride, it later came to light that Hirsch had offered the jockey sparse instruction, telling him basically to do the best he could and offering no advice on use of the whip.

Hirsch was pleased, regardless. It was a good race for

the six-year-old horse, running on his own courage. The race gave Assault the tightener he needed after so long away, and the horse looked fit and ready to run again, which he would do eight days later in the mile and a quarter Brooklyn Handicap.

Assault had won the 1947 Brooklyn handily under 133 pounds. This time he carried a mere 122, receiving seven pounds from top weight Vulcan's Forge, a four-year-old Mahmoud colt who had won the Santa Anita Handicap, Suburban, and Governor's Handicap that year. But Assault, as part of a three-horse King Ranch entry with But Why Not and Flying Missel, was the favorite with Vulcan's Forge the 2-1 second choice. Other major contenders included C.V. Whitney's five-year-old Phalanx, who won the 1947 Belmont Stakes, and Harry LaMontagne's Conniver, a hard-hitting five-year-old daughter of Discovery.

Dave Gorman was aboard Assault for the first time. Eddie Arcaro had committed to other stables when Assault was retired early in 1948 and was aboard Vulcan's Forge. Gorman kept Assault near the early pace, set by the four-year-old colt Three Rings, who went a half in :48 4/5 and six furlongs in 1:13. As

Three Rings tired and the filly Miss Request inherited the lead, Assault took aim as Gorman pointed him home. A roar issued from the crowd of 27,877 at the Big A as Assault launched his bid in the stretch. Vulcan's Forge and Arcaro had been biding their time on the rail but encountered some traffic trouble rounding the second turn. Arcaro angled his charge to the outside, and off they went after Assault. But Gorman rode with confidence as he held the late-closing Vulcan's Forge safe by three-quarters of a length in 2:02 4/5. Vulcan's Forge prevented a one-two finish for King Ranch; Flying Missel, with Assault's old partner Warren Mehrtens up, was only a neck back in third.

The Brooklyn victory made Assault's "comeback" official; "the old man's back" was the word around the backstretch.

"He's the runningest horse I've ever been on," enthused Gorman after the race. With the $40,600 first prize, Assault's earnings totaled $668,020, placing him fourth behind Stymie, Citation, and Armed on the leading money earners list. Citation, the 1948 Triple Crown winner for Calumet Farm, also suffered from an osselet in one ankle and was on the sidelines awaiting his own comeback. Stymie also was sidelined. If Assault's Brooklyn form held, he might have a chance to reclaim the earnings title; he was about $243,000 away.

In early August, Kleberg authorized the entry of Assault and Flying Missel for the October 9 Prix de l'Arc de Triomphe at Longchamp in France. They were the first American-trained entries ever made for the prestigious race. Whether either horse would go depended on many factors, not least of which were how they handled the grass and whether they could stay healthy, especially Assault, who had spent most of his life battling lameness of one sort or another. Of more immediate concern for Assault, as far as Max Hirsch was concerned, was the August 13 Massachusetts Handicap at Suffolk Downs.

The Texas comet was a fresh horse nearly five weeks after the Brooklyn as he prepped for the lucrative MassCap, valued at $50,000-added. In his final serious work, Assault sparkled in a half-mile work in :46 2/5 with Pie Garcia up. He was accompanied by the Hirsch-trained filly Celestia, who received a head start but was run into submission by her stablemate.

His two previous starts combined with the sizzling workout prompted the bettors to back him heavily and he went off at 40 cents on the dollar.

Rain had left the track heavy for the mile and a quarter event but that was not considered a problem as Assault had won on off tracks on three different occasions. Assault also was the top weight at 125 pounds in the five-horse field that included Michigan III, in at 117 pounds, and the lightweights First Nighter, Going Away, and Fancy Flyer. First Nighter, a four-year-old son of Eight Thirty, had won the Lamplighter Handicap the year before.

Fancy Flyer was the early pacesetter with Assault in perfect stalking position on the outside. Assault lost some ground on the first turn but managed to stay close to the pace down the backstretch. Fancy Flyer eventually gave way to Michigan III, then that one relinquished the lead to Going Away. Assault rallied and was only about three-quarters of a length from the lead with a furlong to go when he faltered late. First Nighter, who had trailed early, rushed up along the rail in the stretch to outfinish Going Away by a neck. Michigan III was third, two lengths in front of Assault. After the race

Hirsch discovered the old champion had bled during the running, and Kleberg said he doubted whether Assault would ever run again. But a few days later Hirsch told reporters the bleeding incident was not as bad as originally thought and Assault was doing fine.

"It was a slight hemorrhage — unusual for him — but it could happen to any horse," Hirsch told the Associated Press. Hirsch went on to relate that the bleeding resulted from a broken vein in a nostril and that it stopped soon after the horse reached the barn. "Of course, no matter how slight the bleeding, it stops 'em from running," added the trainer.

Hirsch was stabled at Saratoga and had Assault shipped back there the day after the race, but he didn't plan to run the horse there because there weren't any races for him.

As it turned out, Assault next appeared under tack at Aqueduct for the September 10 Edgemere Handicap. This race was notable for the hoped-for comeback of Stymie, who was making his first start in fourteen months after being sidelined with an injured sesamoid.

Joe Palmer commented in *The Blood-Horse* that Aqueduct's crowded grandstand began to roar with applause when race-goers spotted Stymie's familiar blazed face and high-headed carriage. "It's the sort of thing that feints you into thinking horseplayers are people," Palmer noted wryly. Stymie, who was making his 127th start, remained a beloved favorite with average fans and bettors alike, and his return was highly anticipated, even though trainer Hirsch Jacobs was using the Edgemere more as a tightener and didn't expect him to win.

Not only did Stymie not win, but he finished last in the nine-horse field. As for Assault, he went off the 2-1 favorite and carried top weight of 124 pounds (giving from five to seventeen), but he lacked early speed and trailed for most of the nine-furlong race. He rallied after about seven furlongs and managed to get up for third, three and three-quarters lengths behind the winner, My Request, who had gone wire-to-wire under Eddie Arcaro. With his third-place effort, Assault increased his edge to six to three over Stymie, but this was the first time both had been beaten in the same race.

Next on the agenda for Assault was the Manhattan Handicap on September 24 at Belmont Park. Stymie also was being aimed for the mile and a half race, which he won in 1946 with Assault finishing in a dead heat for third. But this time neither horse could recapture his earlier form. Stymie posed no threat to the leaders and finished a dull fourth, while Assault failed to mount a rally and finished last of seven. Ironically, Warren Mehrtens rode the winner, Donor.

The Manhattan was the last time Assault and Stymie would meet. Like his fellow Texan, Stymie was nearing his own end of a long trail. After the Manhattan, Stymie showed more of his old fire with a second-place finish in the New York Handicap on October 1, but soreness in a leg cut short Stymie's return. Like Assault, he had the heart but not the underpinnings to carry it. As Palmer wrote of Stymie, Assault, and Armed, who also had made a half-hearted return that season: "All three of them came, but not back."

Armed had been away from the races for a year, returning in February 1949. He won three races from twelve starts in 1949 as an eight-year-old, but the wins all came in allowance company, although Armed did place in several stakes. Still, his championship form was long gone.

Stymie retired after the New York Handicap with thirty-five wins in 131 starts and earnings of $918,485. He was not overly successful at stud but did get twelve stakes winners, including the brilliant filly Rare Treat, who won sixteen of 101 starts, among them the 1956 Vineland and 1957 Ladies handicaps. He died in 1962 at age twenty.

With Stymie and Armed both off the track, Assault was the last holdover from their glory days. He had been training fairly well and seemed ready to tackle the October 15 Grey Lag Handicap at Jamaica. However, the Assault who won the Grey Lag two years prior was long gone. In fact, the Assault who had gritted out victory in the Brooklyn earlier that season was long gone. The Assault who ran on that October afternoon settled toward the back of the pack and stayed there, finishing eighth.

It was the second race in a row in which Assault had not even tried to make a run, and some horsemen speculated that the old horse had simply decided not to extend himself in competition anymore because of his old injuries. Other reports indicated he bled again. Regardless of the reason, Assault was retired yet again and sent to King Ranch in Texas.

Kleberg wanted to give Assault another chance at becoming a sire and planned to pasture-breed the horse to some of the farm's Quarter Horse mares. Additional fertility treatments during the spring of 1950 proved futile, though several Quarter Horse mares were reported in foal. As before, Assault had thrived in the mild south Texas fall and winter, and the exercise and fresh air had worked wonders on his health. Kleberg once again decided to put the horse back into training. Assault, now seven, began breezing under tack at King Ranch during the summer.

This time, Assault would head west to the stable of Max Hirsch's son, W.J. (Buddy) Hirsch. Assault made the trip just fine, being shipped by train to Los Angeles, California, but Dr. Monte P. Moncrief, a young veterinarian who along with exercise rider Pie Garcia traveled with the horse, endured a few panic-filled moments on the way.

"We got as far as El Paso on the train when it stopped, and I asked the yardman how long the wait would be," recalled Moncrief. "He said a lengthy time, so I went in to make a phone call."

When Moncrief returned, he found the train had left him. "The train was gone. Gone. A Triple Crown winner on board and no vet," recalled Moncrief. Trying not to panic, the veterinarian chartered a plane and arrived in Los Angeles before the train. Pie Garcia, who also must have been close to panic knowing Moncrief had been left behind, tentatively led Assault down the ramp and looked around. He and the boxcar attendant were both in for a shock when there waiting for them was Moncrief. "What kept you?" he teased.

"My boxcar man's eyes got as big as saucers when he saw me," said Moncrief. "Very few vets get to 'lose' a Triple Crown winner."

Assault arrived at Hollywood Park in mid-October, and temperatures were soaring. Buddy Hirsch warned his father, who was back at King Ranch, that it was above 100 degrees in Southern California, but the elder trainer scoffed, "Only 100? It's more than that inside the ranch house here. Assault won't worry about the heat."

If the heat bothered Assault, he didn't show it, breezing a half-mile in :50 3/5 on October 26. The veteran campaigner looked good — "his solid chestnut flanks gleam in the sunlight," wrote Paul Lowry in the *Los Angeles Times* — and the foot he had injured so long ago, although still misshapen, appeared to be healthier and stronger than ever. Appearance aside, Assault's chances of competing at the top level of the sport were slim, mainly because of his age and all the wear and tear. Still, the seven-year-old horse seemed willing to train and by late November was deemed ready for a race.

Assault made easy work of an allowance field, leading all the way, in an unusual move for him, to win the seven-furlong race by two lengths. Eddie Arcaro, who had ridden him to several major triumphs three years earlier, was aboard for one last time. Arcaro began easing him up when it appeared no one would be challenging, and finished "virtually pulled up," according to the race chart. It was an impressive performance by Assault, particularly because he had not raced in more than a year, was the oldest runner in the field, and carried top weight of 120 pounds. It was the eighteenth victory of his career. And his last hurrah.

Nine days later Assault tried nine furlongs in a prep for the December 9 Hollywood Gold Cup, but this time he weakened in the stretch after making the pace while under pressure from multiple stakes winner Palestinian. But neither horse was any match for the imported powerhouse, Noor, who already had victories over Citation in the Santa Anita Handicap and San Juan Capistrano to his credit that year. With Johnny Longden up, Noor moved into second after six furlongs, then pulled away to win by seven lengths in 1:48. The time clipped a tick off Hollywood Park's track record for a mile and one-eighth.

Afterward, Buddy Hirsch revealed that Assault had bled again, and again retirement beckoned, even though the Gold Cup remained a possibility. "There still is a 50-50 chance that he will go in the Gold Cup," said Hirsch. "But if he does go, that will be the last race of his career."

Assault wasn't the only Triple Crown winner seeking a comeback in 1950. After missing all of 1949 while nursing an injury, the great Citation had returned at five, and although he didn't finish worse than second in his nine starts that year, he couldn't best Noor either, losing to him in the two big Santa Anita races as well as in the Forty-Niner and Golden Gate handicaps. The latter, run June 24, was Citation's last outing in 1950.

He would race again in 1951 and finally reach the elusive million-dollar earnings mark with victory in the Hollywood Gold Cup.

As for the 1950 renewal of the Gold Cup, Assault, who worked a mile and one-eighth in 1:51 three days before the race, faced a daunting challenge if he was to go out with a victory. The eight-horse field was packed with talent — fresh, young talent, in the leading three-year-old colt and filly, Hill Prince and Next Move, respectively. In addition, Noor and Palestinian were running as was Calumet Farm's 1949 Kentucky Derby winner Ponder. For the first time since his two-year-old season, Assault was relegated to longshot status — nearly 38-1.

He ran to his odds. Although he was carried wide on the first turn, Assault rallied to get as close as four and a half lengths off the lead with a furlong to go, but he weakened in the final yards and fell back to finish seventh. Noor closed strongly to win by a length over Palestinian, with Hill Prince third and Next Move fourth. Noor's winning time of 1:59 4/5 was a track record, besting the old record by a fifth of a second. The finish underscored a changing of the guard of sorts.

The old warriors Armed and Stymie had long been retired, Citation had seemingly met his match, and now it was Assault's turn.

Finally, after six seasons of competition, of overcoming various physical problems, of willing himself to victory, Assault was headed home to Texas — this time for good.

CHAPTER 10

Adios, Amigo Mio

A s Assault settled into retired life at King Ranch and with no hope of any sons or daughters, racing fans now cast hopeful eyes toward his siblings for more racetrack glory.

Igual had been bred exclusively to Bold Venture since Assault's birth, but so far the proverbial lightning had not struck twice. Clean Slate, a colt foaled the year after Assault, became stakes-placed but had a wind problem. The promising Air Lift, foaled in 1947, had to be euthanized after breaking an ankle in his first start at two. Then, Mazinga, a 1948 colt, could only manage five seconds in fifteen starts in four seasons of racing. In the spring of 1950, Igual foaled another colt, named Postillion, who would win a couple of minor stakes at age six. Her 1951 foal, the filly On Your Own, managed the best race record of any of Assault's siblings, winning the 1954 Gazelle and Betsy Ross stakes and earning $60,725 from five wins in twenty starts.

But it was Assault's sisters, the winner Sin Igual and the unraced Equal Venture, who did the family most proud. Sin Igual, a 1952 filly, produced the winning Better Self filly Mono, who became the dam of grade III winner A Sure Hit plus two other added-money winners, Rare Performer and Channing Road. Mono's winning daughter Mine Only produced graded stakes winners Academy Award, Statuette, and Good Mood. Statuette and Good Mood both became stakes producers as did another daughter, Chosen Lady, who is the dam of grade I winner Well Chosen and grade III winner In Contention. La Finale, another daughter of Mono, became the dam of grade II winner Ninth Inning.

Equal Venture was the dam of multiple grade I winner Prove Out, the Hobeau Farm runner who upset Secretariat in the 1973 Woodward Stakes, plus stakes winners Saidam and Heartland (dam of grade III winner Distant Land). Prove Out and Heartland were both bred by King Ranch, as were stakes winners Midyan and Harry Hastings (a steeplechaser), both out of Equal Venture's daughter Country Dream (by Ribot). Equal

Venture's daughter Fairness (by Cavan) was the dam of Irish champion miler Solford, graded stakes winner No Bias, and stakes producers No Duplicate, Equal Change, Lagrimas, No Designs, and Ethics. The last-named produced the French group winner Robertet for King Ranch. A daughter of Roberto, Robertet, in turn, produced French group winners Punctilious and Risk Seeker as well as French stakes winner Redwood Falls. No Designs was the dam of Italian group winner Siddharta, who produced Italian champion three-year-old Giovane Imperatore. Equal Change produced the stakes winners Make Change and Spur Wing for King Ranch, while Lagrimas foaled the French stakes winner Hawk Beauty.

Assault and family were only one part of Robert Kleberg's success as a Thoroughbred owner and breeder. In August of 1946, in what would be a momentous decision for King Ranch, Kleberg had the opportunity to acquire some bloodstock from the estate of the late E.R. Bradley. Kleberg joined with influential breeders Ogden Phipps and John Hay Whitney in forming a syndicate to acquire the cream of Bradley's breeding stock. The three men are said to have drawn straws to see who got what; and among the eighteen individuals going to Kleberg were the champions-to-be Bridal Flower and But Why Not as well as a yearling colt by Bimelech—Bee Mac who would be named Better Self, the elder statesman stallion Blue Larkspur, and the broodmares Bee Mac and Be Like Mom (dam of But Why Not).

Kleberg also purchased a 680-acre parcel of the old Idle Hour property located across Old Frankfort Pike from the farm's headquarters (now Darby Dan Farm) in Lexington, Kentucky. Once known as the old Patrick Farm, Kleberg's purchase became King Ranch Kentucky. The farm's proximity to top-class stallions was a major benefit to having a Kentucky farm, but Kleberg always preferred the Texas environment for breeding horses and still bred about 40 percent of his horses there.

"I really feel that with a colt raised in Texas all the way through, that you have a better chance of raising a class horse than you do in Kentucky," he told racing historian and writer Edward L. Bowen in a 1973 interview.

Kleberg died on October 13, 1974, at the age of seventy-eight. He had remained active in the day-to-day management of the ranch, working cattle into his seventies. During the funeral service, an old King Ranch vaquero walked in, tightly gripping his weathered hat. He went over to the open casket and gazed down at his longtime boss. As he turned away, he was heard whispering "adios, amigo mio" (goodbye, my friend), a sign of the deep respect accorded Kleberg by his ranch hands.

Kleberg's passing meant the end of an era for King Ranch, an era that spanned the old and the new. Under his watch, the Santa Gertrudis cattle became a reality and a versatile horse breed was pulled from mediocrity, if not oblivion. From the ranching perspective, he built diversion dams to utilize flood waters and found ways to make brush control more effective and to bring subterranean water to the surface. King Ranch was a leader in soil conservation, and under Caesar Kleberg, the ranch became a leader in wildlife preservation.

But the Thoroughbred brought the Running W to the forefront. Racing devotees who wouldn't have known a Santa Gertrudis from a Jersey certainly knew Assault's name. In the name of King Ranch, Kleberg bred eighty-six stakes winners, including 1950

Kentucky Derby and Belmont winner Middleground; the Coaching Club American Oaks winners Too Timely, Miss Cavandish, and Resaca; and the champion Gallant Bloom.

The Kentucky division of King Ranch continued to thrive under the direction of Kleberg's granddaughter, Helen Alexander. Helen's mother, Helen (Helenita) Groves, had long been an accomplished horsewoman, competing in cutting, as well as breeding and racing Thoroughbreds. The mother and daughter also bred Thoroughbreds together and in other partnerships, including the great filly champion Althea and Aquilegia, Aishah, and Twining, all stakes-winning off-spring from the blue hen mare Courtly Dee, who was acquired by Helen Alexander in partnership. Courtly Dee and her daughters have been very good to Helen Groves and her daughters. Other stakes winners from that family include Aldiza, Bertolini, Aurora, Arch, and Yamanin Paradise.

In 1998 King Ranch Kentucky was sold to Robert N. Clay of Three Chimneys Farm; however, Helen Alexander and her sisters, Emory, Dorothy (Didi), Henrietta, and Caroline remain active in the Thoroughbred industry.

Max Hirsch passed away five years before Kleberg, on April 3, 1969, at age eighty-eight. In between Assault's Triple Crown triumph and Hirsch's death — he never really retired — he sent out forty-six stakes winners, including King Ranch's champions High Gun ("the most underrated horse I ever had"), Gallant Bloom, Bridal Flower, and But Why Not. But Assault held a special place in Hirsch's memories. Of the "Club-footed Comet," Hirsch would say: "Man o' War had everything, but so did Assault; I've never trained a better horse." Another horse who remained special to Hirsch but for an entirely different reason was Stymie — the one who got away. That loss would always rankle Hirsch, who had to watch the horse he bred and sent out for a claiming tag become a champion and leading money earner for someone else.

Not long before he died, the venerable trainer, who had spent more than seventy years in racing, recounted what he had learned about horses, and Stymie was probably uppermost in his thoughts. He said he had learned "not a thing, at least as to how they'll turn out. If people are so smart about horses, how come they pay $100,000 for a yearling that may never get to the post? Horses are a mystery. You can learn how to train a horse and keep improving your methods over the years, like I've done, but you'll never learn how to determine in advance which horse will be good and another bad. It's something inside a horse."

But Hirsch was known not just for his ability to develop good horses, his opinion on that matter notwithstanding, but also for helping jockeys learn the ropes, about both riding and life. At Hirsch's memorial service, Assault's jockey Warren Mehrtens recalled: "Mr. Hirsch taught me everything I know about riding. He kept his eye on the youngsters he had working for him, and one of the things he insisted on was that we go to church every Sunday morning. He was in a class by himself as a horseman and a teacher of kids who wanted to become race riders."

Mehrtens, who thought the world of Hirsch, had been hurt considerably when he was replaced on Assault, but he continued to ride for Hirsch and King Ranch. After showing up at Hirsch's barn one day looking for a job, he was put to work doing routine stable chores, and eventually rose to exercise rider. In August 1940 at Saratoga, Mehrtens rode in his first official race. He retired from riding in 1952 and went to work on the front side as a racing official, working his way up from horse identifier to steward. In 1996 he and his wife, Noreen, visited King Ranch in Texas for the fifti-eth anniversary of Assault's Triple Crown. "He didn't want to go," said Mrs. Mehrtens. "He always hated the limelight but had a good time there." Mehrtens passed away on December 30, 1997, at age seventy-seven.

In his years at King Ranch in Texas, Assault became King Ranch's number one tourist attraction. He would receive fan mail, often addressed just to "Assault, Texas." He also received visits from racing fans who remem-bered his gallant efforts on the racetrack. This author, who was living in Corpus Christi, Texas, at the time, even visited him on numerous occasions. Over the years Assault's exploits seemed to fade from memory until he became a Triple Crown "footnote." People tend to forget that he raced longer and carried more weight than any other Triple Crown winner. But those who knew him would tell you he was no mere "footnote."

Toward the end of his life, Eddie Arcaro recalled the tough little colt: "I rode a lot of great horses. Citation was great. But I would have to put Assault up there with anybody, at least anybody that I ever rode. He wasn't a completely sound horse. I mean, it's a wonder he ever ran to start with. But that's the kind of horse Assault was."[1]

In a 1971 interview with *Dallas Morning News* reporter Randy Galloway, Dr. J.K. Northway, who had saved Assault's life as a foal, remembered his old friend: "He was determined. If he started in one direction and made up his mind to go that way, that's the way he went...This is where he proved his greatness. I don't think there ever has been or ever will be another horse that had the perseverance and the desire of Assault."

Time treats no horse, or man, well. Assault aged as gracefully as time permitted, but inevitably, the years caught up to him. In 1968, when he was twenty-five, King Ranch decided it was time to take Assault out of public view. One last photograph was allowed, then no more. His back had begun to sag a bit; his chestnut coat was graying. He didn't hold his head so high, his ears not so erect. It had been the same with Man o' War at a similar age.

"I want him remembered the way he used to look, not now," Northway told Galloway in their interview.

"...and I'm going to bury him right over there." He pointed to a green lawn, shaded by trees, next to the veterinarian's office.

Ironically after the many leg problems he had endured and overcome, Assault was felled by a paddock accident in which he broke a bone in his left leg near the shoulder. He was euthanized on September 1, 1971, at age twenty-eight. With his death the lone surviving Triple Crown winner at that time was Count Fleet, the 1943 winner, who was thirty-one. Assault was buried at King Ranch in the place Northway had indicated, with Middleground and several Quarter Horse champions. Assault was laid to rest with his head facing west and, in the old cavalry position, with his legs positioned as though he were running. His resting spot is marked by a simple stone, giving the basics — his name, pedigree, and birth and death dates — plus his public crowning glory: Triple Crown winner 1946.

Assault's extraordinary accomplishments could never fit on a gravestone, though. Nothing ever came easily for the little chestnut with the bad foot, but a heart as big as Texas helped Assault prevail over adversity to achieve a singular greatness.

And on moonlight nights one can almost see a phantom herd of mustangs running across the Wild Horse Desert. Now they are led by a small chestnut Thoroughbred...Adios, amigo mio.

ASSAULT's
PEDIGREE

BOLD VENTURE, ch, 1933	St. Germans, 1921	Swynford, 1907	John o' Gaunt Canterbury Pilgrim
		Hamoaze, 1911	Torpoint Maid of the Mist
	Possible, 1920	Ultimus, 1906	Commando Running Stream
ASSAULT, chestnut colt, 1943		Lida Flush, 1910	Royal Flush III Lida H.
	Equipoise, 1928	Pennant, 1911	Peter Pan Royal Rose
		Swinging, 1922	Broomstick Balancoire II
IGUAL, ch, 1937	Incandescent, 1931	Chicle, 1913	Spearmint Lady Hamburg II
		Masda, 1915	Fair Play Mahubah

ASSAULT's RACE RECORD

Assault — ch. c. 1943, by Bold Venture (St. Germans)–Igual, by Equipoise — Lifetime record: 42 18 6 7 $675,470

Own.– King Ranch
Br.– King Ranch (Tex)
Tr.– W.J. Hirsch

9Dec50- 7Hol	fst	1¼	:46^{3} 1:10^{1} 1:35 1:59^{4}	3↑ Hol Gold Cup 137k	5	2	5^{3½}	5^{3¾}	4^{4½}	7^{10¼}	Gilbert J	121wb	37.95	91-09	Noor130^{1}Palestinian122^{3}Hill Prince130^{1}		8
	Carried wide,rallied,flattened out																
1Dec50- 7Hol	fst	1⅛	:48 1:11^{4} 1:36^{1} 1:48	3↑ Alw 5000	1	1	2^{hd}	1½	2^{3}	3^{8}	Boland W	112wb	1.90	93-11	Noor124^{7}Palestinian120^{1}Assault112^{1}	Weakened	5
22Nov50- 7Hol	fst	7f	:22^{2} :45^{1} 1:09^{3} 1:22^{4}	3↑ Alw 4000	1	1	1^{1½}	1^{2½}	1^{4}	1^{2}	Arcaro E	120wb	2.90	95-16	Assault120^{2}Repeluz116^{2}Bernbrook113^{1}	Easing up	7
	Previously trained by M. Hirsch																
15Oct49- 6Jam	fst	1$\frac{1}{16}$	:24^{2} :48 1:12^{4} 1:44^{2}	3↑ Grey Lag H 29k	10	8	8^{7¼}	8^{5}	8^{4¼}	8^{6¼}	Arcaro E	123wb	4.75e	85-16	Royal Governor114^{1}Three Rings116^{hd}Capot121^{nk}	No rally	12
24Sep49- 6Bel	fst	1½	:49 1:13 2:02^{2} 2:28	3↑ Manhattan H 29k	7	4	6^{6}	6^{11}	7^{9¼}	7^{14}	Gorman D	126wb	*2.15	84-13	Donor118¾My Request125^{8}Stunts114^{hd}	Wide,outrun	7
10Sep49- 6Aqu	fst	1⅛	:47^{3} 1:12 1:37 1:50^{4}	3↑ Edgemere H 22k	3	9	9^{16}	9^{14}	4^{8½}	3^{3¾}	Gorman D	124wb	*2.50	89-16	My Request119^{3}Stunts115¾Assault124½	Closed fast	9
13Aug49- 7Suf	hy	1¼	:48^{2} 1:13^{3} 1:39^{3} 2:04^{3}	3↑ Mass H 59k	5	2	2^{1}	3¾	3¾	4^{3}	Gorman D	125wb	*.40	87-27	FirstNighter104^{nk}GoingAway103¾MichgnIII117^{2}	Lost ground	5
2Jly49- 6Aqu	fst	1¼	:48^{4} 1:13 1:37^{2} 2:02^{4}	3↑ Brooklyn H 58k	7	5	4^{2}	2½	1^{1½}	1¾	Gorman D	122wb	*.95e	93-14	Assault122¾Vulcan's Forge129^{nk}Flying Missel117¾	Driving	10
24Jun49- 5Aqu	fst	7f	:23^{1} :46 1:12 1:26^{2}	4↑ Alw 4000	4	2	3^{2}	1½	1^{hd}	2no	Boland W	119wb	*.35	80-27	Michigan III115^{no}Assault119^{4}Spats108^{2}	Weak ride	5
21Feb48- 6Hia	fst	1¼	:47 1:11 1:35^{4} 2:01	3↑ Widener H 62k	1	5	8^{5¾}	3^{1}	4^{2¼}	5^{7}	Arcaro E	130wb	*1.15	96-10	El Mono112^{hd}Stud Poker103^{2½}Bug Juice107^{3}	Faltered	9
14Feb48- 5Hia	fst	7f	:23^{3} :47 1:11^{3} 1:23^{4}	4↑ Alw 5000	1	4	3^{3}	2^{1½}	2½	1^{hd}	Mehrtens W	126wb	*.40	93-10	Assault128^{hd}Rampart109^{7}Star Pilot116^{9}	Not urged	4
27Sep47- 6Bel	fst	1¼	:47^{1} 1:11^{3} 1:36^{3} 2:02^{4}	3↑ Special 100k	1	2	2^{4}	2^{2}	2^{3}	2^{8}	Arcaro E	126wb	-	78-10	Armed126^{8}Assault126	Outrun	2
19Jly47- 6Bel	sly	1⅝	:48^{3} 1:39 2:04^{2} 2:42^{3}	3↑ Gold Cup 109k	2	2	4^{18}	4^{5½}	2^{1½}	3^{4¼}	Arcaro E	126wb	*.55	87-14	Stymie126^{nk}Natchez126^{4}Assault126^{1}	Swerved,tired	7
	Geldings not eligible																
12Jly47- 5Jam	fst	1$\frac{3}{16}$	:49 1:13^{4} 1:38^{1} 1:56^{3}	3↑ Butler H 54k	5	2	4^{5}	4^{4½}	5^{1}	1^{hd}	Arcaro E	135wb	*.45	93-09	Assault135^{hd}Stymie126^{1¾}Gallorette117^{nk}	Hard drive	5
21Jun47- 6Aqu	fst	1¼	:47^{2} 1:12^{1} 1:38 2:03^{3}	3↑ Brooklyn H 55k	2	1	4^{14}	4^{5½}	2½	1^{3}	Arcaro E	133wb	*.45	89-14	Assault133^{3}Stymie124^{4}Larky Day110^{1}	Easily	5
30May47- 6Bel	fst	1¼	:47^{2} 1:11^{4} 1:36^{4} 2:01^{4}	3↑ Suburban H 57k	2	4	4^{6½}	2^{6}	2^{1½}	1^{2}	Arcaro E	130wb	*1.10	91-09	Assault130^{2}Natchez120^{7}Talon113^{1}	Going away	7
9May47- 6Pim	fst	1$\frac{3}{16}$	:47^{4} 1:12^{2} 1:38^{4} 1:57^{4}	3↑ Dixie H 35k	7	1	5^{6½}	5^{4¼}	2^{hd}	1½	Arcaro E	129wb	*.40e	93-20	Assault129½Rico Monte120^{3}Talon115^{2}	Hand ride	7
3May47- 5Jam	fst	1⅛	:47 1:11^{2} 1:36^{3} 1:49^{4}	3↑ Grey Lag H 46k	2	6	6^{8½}	4^{1½}	4^{nk}	1^{nk}	Mehrtens W	128wb	*1.25	99-13	Asslt128^{nk}LetsDanc110^{nk}Concdnc120^{2}	Bumped,forced wide	8
	Daily Racing Form time,1:49 1/5																
9Nov46- 5Jam	gd	1$\frac{3}{16}$	:47^{2} 1:11^{2} 1:37^{3} 1:56^{2}	3↑ Westchester H 56k	4	5	6^{9½}	5^{10}	1^{1½}	1^{2}	Arcaro E	122wb	1.65	94-17	Assault122^{2½}Lucky Draw128^{4}Lets Dance104^{1½}	Cleverly	6
1Nov46- 6Pim	fst	1$\frac{3}{16}$	:48^{1} 1:13^{2} 1:39 1:57	3↑ Pim Spl 25k	3	3	3^{14}	3^{9½}	1^{1}	1^{6}	Arcaro E	120wb	2.80	97-16	Assault120^{6}Stymie126^{3}Bridal Flower117½	Easily	4
26Oct46- 5Jam	fst	1⅝	:46^{2} 1:37^{3} 2:03 2:42^{4}	3↑ Gallant Fox H 85k	10	6	5^{7½}	1^{1}	3^{5½}	3^{4½}	Mehrtens W	114wb	4.90	96-11	Stymie126^{2½}Rico Monte116^{2}Assault114^{8}	Weakened	11
19Oct46- 5Jam	fst	1$\frac{3}{16}$	:47^{3} 1:12^{3} 1:39 1:57^{2}	Roamer H 31k	7	11	9^{6¾}	7^{5¼}	2^{nk}	2½	Mehrtens W	126wb	*1.40	88-13	Bridal Flower118½Assault126^{1½}Risolater109^{nk}	Hung	12
25Sep46- 6Bel	fst	1½	:49^{3} 1:14^{3} 2:03^{2} 2:29^{2}	3↑ Manhattan H 28k	2	3	5^{4¼}	5^{3¾}	4^{4¾}	3^{3¾}♦	Mehrtens W	116wb	1.90	87-13	Stymie126¾Pavot121^{3}[DH]Flareback113^{1}	Came on again	8
14Sep46- 5GS	fst	1⅛	:47^{2} 1:12^{1} 1:36^{3} 1:49^{1}	Jersey H 31k	5	6	6^{5½}	3^{1}	2^{hd}	2½	Mehrtens W	126wb	*.70	98-09	Mahout114½Assault126^{3}Blue Yonder113^{1¼}	No excuse	7
7Sep46- 6Aqu	fst	1⅛	:48 1:12^{3} 1:39 1:51^{4}	Discovery H 28k	4	8	8^{12}	6^{7}	5^{7¼}	3^{3½}	Mehrtens W	126wb	*.70e	84-14	Mighty Story115^{2½}Mahout112^{1}Assault126¾	Forced wide	9
27Jly46- 6AP	fst	1¼	:49^{1} 1:12^{3} 1:36^{4} 2:02^{3}	Classic 94k	2	2	3^{3½}	4^{8½}	6^{10½}	6^{8¼}	Mehrtens W	126wb	*.70	85-09	The Dude119^{1¼}Sgt. Spence119^{2½}Mighty Story122^{2}	Sulked	6
15Jun46- 6Aqu	fst	1¼	:48^{1} 1:14 1:41^{1} 2:06^{4}	Dwyer 58k	6	4	5^{9¼}	3^{3½}	2^{nk}	1^{4½}	Mehrtens W	126wb	*.40	73-23	Assault126^{4½}Windfields116½Lord Boswell121^{1½}	Easily	6
1Jun46- 6Bel	fst	1½	:49^{3} 1:14^{1} 2:04 2:30^{4}	Belmont 110k	1	7	4^{5¼}	3^{3½}	3^{2}	1^{3}	Mehrtens W	126wb	1.40	84-13	Assault126^{3}Natchez126^{2}Cable126^{hd}	Going away	7
	Geldings not eligible																

ASSAULT's RACE RECORD CONTINUED

11May46- 6Pim	fst $1\frac{3}{16}$	:48	1:13	1:40	$2{:}01^{2}$	Preakness 131k	5	6	6^{5}	$3\frac{1}{2}$	1^{4}	1^{nk}	Mehrtens W	126wb	*1.40	75-20	$Assault126^{nk}Lord Boswell126^{3\frac{1}{2}}Hampden126^{4}$	Ridden out 10
4May46- 7CD	sl $1\frac{1}{4}$	:48	$1{:}14^{1}$	$1{:}40^{4}$	$2{:}06^{3}$	Ky Derby 113k	2	3	5^{4}	3^{2}	$1^{2\frac{1}{2}}$	1^{8}	Mehrtens W	126wb	8.20	74-22	$Assault126^{8}Spy Song126^{hd}Hampden126^{1}$	Drew away 17
30Apr46- 5CD	my 1	$:22^{3}$	$:46^{3}$	$1{:}12^{3}$	$1{:}40^{1}$	Derby Trial 13k	5	5	4^{10}	$4^{7\frac{1}{2}}$	$4^{7\frac{1}{2}}$	$4^{4\frac{1}{2}}$	Mehrtens W	118wb	4.50	73-32	$Rippey110^{nk}Spy Song118^{4}With Pleasure118^{nk}$	Closed ground 10
20Apr46- 5Jam	fst $1\frac{1}{16}$	$:23^{3}$	:47	$1{:}11^{3}$	$1{:}46^{3}$	Wood Memorial 31k	11	3	3^{5}	3^{4}	2^{hd}	$1^{2\frac{1}{4}}$	Mehrtens W	126wb	8.85	80-18	$Assault126^{2\frac{1}{4}}Hampden126^{\frac{1}{2}}Marine Victory126^{1}$	Going away 14
	Daily Racing Form time,1:47 1/5																	
9Apr46- 5Jam	fst 6f	:23	:47		1:12	Exp Free H 11k	6	6	$3^{1\frac{1}{2}}$	$1^{\frac{1}{2}}$	1^{3}	$1^{4\frac{1}{2}}$	Mehrtens W	116wb	9.10	91-17	$Assault116^{4\frac{1}{2}}Islam Prince114^{\frac{1}{2}}Larkmead Andy110^{nk}$	Hand ride 11
8Oct45- 5Jam	fst 6f	:23	$:46^{3}$		1:12	Alw 5000	4	5	$4^{3\frac{1}{4}}$	3^{1}	2^{hd}	2^{3}	Mehrtens W	117wb	2.15	89-15	$Lord Boswell117^{3}Assault117^{4}Landlord111^{2\frac{1}{2}}$	No match 5
12Sep45- 6Aqu	fst $6\frac{1}{2}$f	$:23^{1}$	$:46^{4}$	$1{:}12^{2}$	1:18	Cowdin 31k	8	9	11^{7}	8^{8}	$5^{4\frac{1}{2}}$	4^{4}	Mehrtens W	120wsb	34.40	91-14	$Knockdown114^{1\frac{1}{2}}Revokd126^{1}SouthernPrd120^{1\frac{1}{2}}$	Finished well 13
5Sep45- 6Aqu	fst 6f	$:22^{3}$	$:46^{3}$		$1{:}12^{1}$	Babylon H 14k	6	6	$3^{1\frac{1}{4}}$	2^{1}	2^{1}	3^{4}	Mehrtens W	119wb	10.90	87-17	$Southern Pride120^{1}Tidy Bid113^{3}Assault119^{nk}$	Hung 9
6Aug45- 4Bel	sly $5\frac{1}{2}$f-W	$:22^{1}$	$:45^{2}$		$1{:}04^{4}$	Flash 15k	11	1		2^{nk}	$4^{2\frac{3}{4}}$	1no	Mehrtens W	113wb	70.60	90-10	$Assault113^{no}Mist o' Gold122^{no}Mush Mush117^{hd}$	Driving 12
18Jly45- 5Jam	fst 6f	:23	$:46^{1}$		$1{:}12^{1}$	©East View 12k	1	5	$5^{3\frac{3}{4}}$	$4^{5\frac{1}{2}}$	$5^{3\frac{1}{2}}$	$5^{8\frac{1}{2}}$	Mehrtens W	118 w	18.05	82-15	$Misto'Gold122^{1\frac{1}{2}}SouthrnPride118^{3}Degage122^{2}$	Saved ground 14
12Jly45- 5Aqu	fst $5\frac{1}{2}$f	$:22^{3}$	$:46^{3}$		$1{:}07^{2}$	©Alw 3000	2	2	1^{hd}	2^{1}	$2^{\frac{1}{2}}$	$1^{1\frac{1}{4}}$	Mehrtens W	111wb	4.65	87-19	$Assault111^{1\frac{1}{4}}Happy C.116^{\frac{3}{4}}Darby Darius116^{1\frac{1}{4}}$	7
	Saved ground,ridden out																	
23Jun45- 2Bel	fst $4\frac{1}{2}$f-W	$:23^{1}$	$:46^{4}$		:53	©Md Sp Wt	16	3		$1^{1\frac{1}{2}}$	2^{1}	2^{3}	Mehrtens W	116wb	23.95	87-12	$Mist o' Gold116^{3}Assault116^{1}Uncle Mac116^{1\frac{1}{2}}$	No mishap 23
12Jun45- 1Bel	fst $4\frac{1}{2}$f-W	$:25^{1}$	$:47^{1}$		$:53^{3}$	©Md Sp Wt	12	4		$4^{\frac{3}{4}}$	$6^{2\frac{3}{4}}$	$5^{1\frac{3}{4}}$	Mehrtens W	116 w	79.25	85-12	$Leeway109^{hd}Challenge Play116^{1\frac{1}{2}}The Heir116^{hd}$	Early speed 15
4Jun45- 4Bel	sly $4\frac{1}{2}$f-W	$:22^{4}$	$:46^{2}$		$:53^{1}$	©Md Sp Wt	13	8		11^{8}	11^{14}	$12^{14\frac{1}{2}}$	Stout J	116 w	17.30	74-13	$Grandpa Max116^{4}The Heir116^{1\frac{1}{2}}Skylighter116^{1}$	Evenly 21

References

Introduction

1. Lea, Tom. *The King Ranch*. Vol. I. Boston: Little, Brown (1957), p. 434.

Chapter 4

1. Personal letter from Robert Kleberg Jr. to Max Hirsch, Queens, New York. September 20, 1943. Courtesy of the King Ranch Archives.
2. Orchard, Julie. "The Three-Footed Miracle." *American Farriers Journal*. May/June 1996. p. 77.
3. Simon, Mary. *Racing Through the Century: The Story of Thoroughbred Racing in America*. Irvine, Calif.: Bowtie Press (2002), p. 127.

Chapter 6

1. Cooke, Bob. "Max Hirsch 'Belonged'." *Horsemen's Journal*. April 1982. pp. 42–43.
2. Rees, Jennie. "Assault: Three good legs and one Triple Crown." Louisville *Courier-Journal*. April 28, 1996.
3. Koper, George. "Mehrtens' First Derby Ride was Winner." Louisville *Courier-Journal*. May 5, 1946.
4. Dollins is quoted in several sources, including Richard Tijerina. "Texas' Triple Crown Connection." *Corpus Christi Caller-Times*. May 3, 1996.
5. Koper. "Mehrtens' First Derby Ride Was Winner."
6. Renneisen, Richard. "Kleberg Proud that Assault is Texas-bred." Louisville *Courier-Journal*. May 5, 1946.
7. Ibid.
8. Amon, Harry. "Assault's Happy Trainer Accepts Governor's Salute to Texas." Louisville *Courier-Journal*, May 5, 1946.
9. McNerney, Jerry. "Assault, Son of a Derby Victor, Wins by 8." Louisville *Courier-Journal*, May 5, 1946.

Chapter 7

1. Tijerina. "Texas' Triple Crown Connection."
2. Bolus, Jim. *Derby Magic*. Gretna, La.: Pelican Publishing Co. (1997), p. 64.
3. Bolus. Ibid.
4. Tijerina. Ibid.
5. Palmer, Joe H. *American Race Horses of 1946*. Belair, Md.: Sagamore Press (1947), p. 72.
6. Palmer. Ibid.

Chapter 8

1. Palmer, Joe H. *American Race Horses of 1947.* Belair, Md.: Sagamore Press (1948), p. 46.

2. Ibid. p. 47.

3. Ibid.

4. Tijerina. "Texas' Triple Crown Connection."

Chapter 10

1. Tijerina. "Texas' Triple Crown Connection."

Index

ACKNOWLEDGMENTS

I owe so much to so many I don't know where to start. The best place would be to God. He has kept me going this year when it appeared *Assault* would not even get out of the starting gate.

I can't say enough about my editor, Jacqueline Duke of Eclipse Press, who was patient and understanding as one setback after another kept me from deadline. To Jackie, managing editor Judy Marchman, and the Eclipse Press staff, thank you for sticking with me and trusting me. I hope *Assault* doesn't disappoint you.

Many thanks to Dusty Knoblauch and Lisa Neely. Dusty is a tour guide at King Ranch and is specially knowledge-able about the Thoroughbred era. She took me on the "Assault" tour, showing me the colt's world, from where he was born, where his life was saved, and where he rests today. As archivist for King Ranch, Lisa pulled countless records from the archives and copied them for my use in the book. She also introduced me to Dr. Monte Moncrief who shared with me tidbits from the life of a Triple Crown winner, and also to Lolo Treviño, whose gentle hands as a youngster were among the first to tame Assault's spirit and teach him the ways of a proper racehorse. I also want to thank Mrs. Helen Groves who shared her memories of Assault with me.

No book involving research on racehorses can be successful without the aid of the Keeneland Library. Librarians Cathy Schenck and Phyllis Rogers were always eager to supply me with whatever material I needed.

Dorothy Ours at the National Museum of Racing is another who was always ready to supply me with information from the museum's vast resources. Thank you, Dee.

And I cannot fail to thank Dr. Foster and the nurses and aides on the seventh floor of Sid Peterson Memorial Hospital in Kerrville, Texas, who put up with my "wait a minute, I need to finish this paragraph..." All were incredibly tolerant of all my papers scattered over the bed, bed table, and even the chair meant to accommodate my broken hip. In addition, the staff at AmeriPark Care Center in Kerrville were kind enough to allow me to use their office and fax machine. Also, I want to thank Sherry Strain, my pastor at St. Paul's United Methodist Church in Kerrville, for all of her help and support.

And lastly but in no way the least, thank you Laura Hillenbrand for your support and the inspiration you've shown in your wonderful *Seabiscuit*.

Eva Jolene Boyd

Photo Credits

Cover photo: (The Blood-Horse)

Page 1: Assault conformation (Bert Clark Thayer); Assault with Robert Kleberg Jr. (Courtesy King Ranch Archives, King Ranch Inc., Kingsville, Texas)

Page 2: Bold Venture (The Blood-Horse); St. Germans (J.A. Estes); Igual (Skeets Meadors); Equipoise (The Blood-Horse)

Page 3: Helenita Kleberg and Assault (Bert Clark Thayer); Max Hirsch, Mr. & Mrs. Robert Kleberg, Eddie Arcaro, and A.G. Vanderbilt (Maryland Jockey Club); Arcaro and Hirsch (The Blood-Horse)

Page 4: Warren Mehrtens and Assault (The Blood-Horse); Mehrtens with Preakness trophy (The Blood-Horse); Arcaro and Assault (Bert Morgan); Dave Gorman and Assault (New York Racing Association)

Page 5: Assault winning the Experimental Handicap No. 1 (Bert Morgan); Winning the Wood Memorial (The Blood-Horse); Assault's bad foot (Courtesy King Ranch Archives)

Page 6-7: Winning the Kentucky Derby (Courier-Journal and Louisville Times); Derby winner's circle (Bert Morgan); Derby trophy presentation (Kinetic)

Page 8: Winning the Preakness (Bert Morgan); Preakness winner's circle (The Blood-Horse)

Page 9: Winning the Belmont (Bert Morgan); Belmont winner's circle (NYRA)

Page 10: Winning the Pimlico Special (Maryland Jockey Club); Winning the Westchester (Bert Morgan); Assault in stall (University of Louisville Photo Archives)

Page 11: Winning the Grey Lag (Bert Morgan); Dixie Handicap winner's circle (Pimlico); Dixie trophy presentation (Pimlico)

Page 12: Winning the Suburban (Bert Morgan); Winning the Brooklyn (NYRA); Winning the Butler Handicap (Bert Morgan)

Page 13: Assault arrives in Hialeah (The Blood-Horse); Assault works at Hialeah (The Blood-Horse)

Page 14: Winning the Mimosa Purse (The Blood-Horse); Winning the 1949 Brooklyn (NYRA); Winning Hollywood Park allowance (Courtesy King Ranch Archives)

Page 15: "Assault" baseball park (Eva Jolene Boyd); Main residence (Courtesy King Ranch Archives)

Page 16: Assault at King Ranch (Eva Jolene Boyd); Gravestone (The Blood-Horse)

ABOUT THE
AUTHOR

Eva Jolene Boyd is a sixth-generation Texan. Born in San Antonio in 1937, she has loved horses her entire life. Assault was the first great racehorse she ever saw in person when she went to King Ranch, so she considers it an honor to pen his biography.

Boyd's love affair with Thoroughbred racing began in 1953 when she saw the telecast of Native Dancer winning the Gotham Stakes.

She eventually combined her love for both horses and writing. She has had articles published in *The Thoroughbred Record*, *Turf and Sport Digest*, *SPUR*, *The Backstretch*, and *The Blood-Horse*.

In addition to *Assault*, Boyd is the author of two other Thoroughbred Legends titles, *Native Dancer* and *Exterminator*, as well as *That Old Overland Stagecoaching*, and *Noble Brutes: Camels on the American Frontier*. She resides in Ingram, Texas.